**New Approaches to State
Land-Use Policies**

New Approaches to State Land-Use Policies

Melvin R. Levin
Rutgers University

Jerome G. Rose
Rutgers University

Joseph S. Slavet
University of Massachusetts

Lexington Books
D.C. Heath and Company
Lexington, Massachusetts
Toronto   London

Library of Congress Cataloging in Publication Data

Levin, Melvin R.   1924-
 New approaches to state land use policies.

 1. Land—United States. 2. Land—New Jersey. 3. State governments. I. Rose, Jerome G., joint author. II. Slavet, Joseph S., joint
author. III. Title.
HD205   1974.L48   333.1'0973   74-13735
ISBN 0-669-96149-3

Contents

Preface

In recent years states have begun to play a more active role in land-use planning. To a degree, the emergence of state leadership in this field is linked to the decline of federal initiatives, which began in the late 1960s, and after much rhetoric, blossomed into the near rigor mortis (in the planning area) during the second Nixon administration. This federal paralysis left the more imaginative states with no option but to act on their own, a dramatic reversal of the situation of a generation earlier in the Great Depression. At that time, the federal government was forced to take up the slack for those states that had proved reluctant to meet the needs of their populations.

In actuality, governments have never really been absent from the land-development process: state-planned highway systems and, to a lesser extent, other state facilities, such as parks and beaches, colleges, and technical schools, have traditionally been major elements in the framework within which land-use decisions are made. But the key factors in urban development are the private sector (owner, developer, and financier) and the municipalities.

A pervasive sense of dissatisfaction has emerged with this traditional process. Too many municipalities have made a hash of their land use patterns, partly through poor-quality planning and partly because of the practice of zoning by exception: community zoning barriers have proven weak defenses against developers urging—and getting—parcel-by-parcel special variances.

In the broader sense, municipal control over land use has created serious problems. These include the creation of innumerable hazard-creating roadside swathes of strip development; preemption of open space, which includes the private purchase of waterfront property; and the widespread practice of exclusionary zoning in sizable metropolitan territories. After observing the accumulated results of home rule applied to land use, in an era of heightened sensitivity to the environment, increased affluence, and higher education levels, a number of states have moved to protect their land-use resources. Some of the pioneering states, such as Vermont, are still largely open and rural. Others (such as California, Florida, and Hawaii) contain both major urban areas and highly productive farmland. Some others, Massachusetts and New Jersey, for example, are heavily urbanized. What all of these states have in common is a response to the recognition that the present pattern of fragmented land-use regulation poses a threat to the preservation of land-use resources vital to their future.

New Jersey finds itself in a particularly difficult position. Most of the state functions as a brief—90 mile—segment of the 400 mile Boston-Washington megalopolis. Waves of suburban growth emanating from the massive metropolitan New York and Philadelphia areas have inundated the northeast and south central portions of New Jersey. Moreover, this overspill has taken a special form. While it has received its share of middle- and upper-income residential subdivisions, research parks, and regional shopping centers, New Jersey has also been the recipient of enormous quantities of noxious industries. The outstanding example is petroleum refining: New Jersey now contains one-third of the entire refining capacity of the Maine-to-Florida coastal states and, if current expansion plans reach fruition, the proportion will rise to two-thirds of the total.

The enormous extent of the preemption and pollution of its coastal and wetland zones has been partly responsible for New Jersey's leadership in developing programs for protecting environmentally sensitive areas. Sadly, much of the response has been too little and too late: most of the once-attractive shorefront, including magnificent sand dunes and wetlands, has been given over to miles of honky-tonk piers and thousands of tract houses. It is an instructive commentary on the state-of-the-action that New Jersey's last ditch defense of its remaining resources is nonetheless a pioneering effort.

This monograph is the tangible product of a study sponsored by New Jersey's Department of Community Affairs. Although initially the research focused primarily on the significant neglected problem of the peripheral land-use impacts related to Planned Unit Developments (of which New Jersey has dozens in the planning and proposal stage), it quickly became apparent that both a viable state land-use policy and effective regulation are prerequisites for coping with intermunicipal land-use issues—the counties are unequal to the task; there is no reasonable prospect of regional governmental entities with substantial land-use powers; and the municipalities are responsible for many of our present difficulties. By default, this challenging task is thus left to the state.

The study examines existing New Jersey land-use legislation and proceeds to an analysis of land-use planning in a number of states that have been leaders in the field. The concluding chapter proposes an administrative approach tailored to New Jersey's special needs. In addition, there is an Appendix devoted to proposed "development rights" legislation, an interesting technique whereby states can encourage municipalities to set aside large amounts of permanent open space without requiring governmental expenditure for costly land aquisition.

One element in the proposed New Jersey model is clearly applicable to other states: past experience shows that if an agency entrusted with critical coordinative land-use responsibilities is to be effective, it must be in a *superordinate* position; it cannot function successfully as an equal attempting to persuade powerful sister agencies (for example, the highway department) to relate functional planning and construction activities to broad land-use goals. The final chapter discusses alternative ways of providing the state land-use agency with this status. But whatever the organizational choice, the history of state planning in New Jersey and other states indicates that there must be substantial financing and staffing. In far too many instances, legislative enactments with laudable goals and ringing preambles have been crippled by the absence of such banal prerequisites for enforcement as operating funds and trained staff. And most important, particularly in the formative stages, there must be vigorous, tough, dedicated leadership. There is no surer road to disappointment than turning over top positions in new agencies to tired bureaucrats, aged and dessicated by too many years and too many losing battles, prone to conjure up frightening problems for every solution.

Perhaps the most important ingredient is tenacity—the ability to persevere despite opposition, complaints, law suits, and formidable political pressures. The study touches on the manifold problems already encountered on several land-use fronts, including the opposition besetting fair housing legislation, the pros and cons of construction moratoriums, and the resistance to protection of coastal areas from urban development. The list of difficulties is endless and for this reason, in political terms, a policy combining drift and planning pageantry, high-minded, long-winded conferences with acquiescence to developer initiatives, can be more comfortable than unsettling activism.

Unfortunately, a passive governmental posture will lead to disaster. In less than a generation, little of New Jersey (or indeed of other urbanized states) will remain habitable by any reasonable standard unless there is an effective state planning mechanism. If justification is needed for taking what appears to be dangerous political risks, one should consider the alternative, which is even more horrendous. Indeed, it is not inconceivable that after a decade or two we may witness a powerful trend toward abandonment of major parts of environmentally degraded states, just as we have seen wholesale abandonment of sizable slum areas of central cities.

There are some who believe that the ball game in New Jersey is over and that the future holds nothing in store but more of the same: that is, state government will huff and puff but will essentially stand aside from a development process that will lead to more urban sprawl, continued reliance on regressive local property taxes, more disjointed strip development, more low-quality subdivisions, more environmental degradation. This grim forecast is based on a simple assumption: other states may find it possible to take their land-use future into their hands, but New Jersey is a terminal case: politically retarded, congealed, and fossilized, its fate sealed by a fatal brew of history, economics, and technology. Taking this a step further, it is argued that while each new state administration recognizes the seriousness of the land-use problem in its campaign rhetoric and party platform, subsequent preliminary grapplings with thorny issues like home rule and confrontations with prodevelopment legislative blocs make it extremely unlikely that glowing promises will be matched by substantive performance.

Certainly, past history provides ample cause for cynicism and despair, but it also offers further reason for redoubled efforts to save New Jersey's oases, the few neighborhoods, towns, and unspoiled open spaces that have so far resisted creeping blight. But there are also grounds for believing that New Jersey can advance beyond a *sauve qui peut* philosophy. Many New Jersey communities have learned that headlong development for the sake of tax ratables is often reckless and self-defeating. Many are beginning to learn that reputable developers will respond to higher standards and that land values rise as a consequence of a policy of selection and direction rather than one of simple acquiescence to developer proposals. And most of all, they have learned the clear, pragmatic lesson that good planning saves pain, grief, and costly corrective expenditures.

As this report indicates, New Jersey has been a leader in environmental legislation. The question now is whether this leadership can be extended to all of the Garden State's land-use resources. New Jersey's success or failure in this endeavor will provide valuable lessons for other states throughout the nation.

Melvin R. Levin
New Bruswick, N.J.
June 1974

Acknowledgment

This study is based on a report prepared for the New Jersey Department of Community Affairs with financial aid from the U.S. Department of Housing and Urban Development. The authors wish to thank members of the Department of Community Affairs for their review and helpful comments. The opinions expressed in the study, however, are those of the authors and do not necessarily reflect the views of DCA staff.

1   Introduction

This study arose from the need to develop state policy relating to the land-use spillover effects of planned unit developments (PUDs)[a] and new communities[b] in New Jersey. This type of impact is emerging as an increasingly important problem because, by mid-1973, there were more than 80 PUDs in the planning and construction stage in New Jersey, along with active proposals for the development of six new communities. The overall impact of this pattern can be gauged from the fact that this volume of construction is likely to account for at least 10 percent of total residential construction throughout the state during the 1970-1980 decade. Equally important, the construction of these planned developments is bound to have a major impact on residential construction throughout New Jersey, but most particularly in the areas immediately contiguous to PUDs and new communities.

The peripheral consequences of land-use spillover of major developments tend to be overlooked, a neglect that is in stark contrast to the highly professional and intensive planning that goes into the conceptualization and implementation of the PUDs and the new communities proper. Since the public and private advantages of

---

[a]PUDs are defined as follows in a recent monograph:

Planned unit development is a means of land regulation which promotes large scale, unified land development via mid-range, realizable programs in pursuit of physically-curable, social and economic deficiencies in peripheral land and cityscapes. Where appropriate this development control advocates: (1) A mixture of both land uses and dwelling types, one or more of the non-residential land uses being regional in nature. (2) The clustering of residential land uses providing public and common open space, the latter to be maintained for and by the residents of the development. (3) Increased administrative discretion to a local professional planning staff while setting aside preset land use regulations and rigid plat approval processes, and finally, (4) The enhancement of the bargaining processes, between developer and municipality thereby strengthening the municipality's site plan review function and control over tempo and sequence of development in return for potentially increased profits available to the developer as a result of land efficiency, the employment of multiple land uses, and increased residential densities. [From Robert W. Burchell, *Planned Unit Development: New Communities American Style* (New Brunswick, N.J.: Center for Urban Policy Research, Rutgers University, 1972), p. 37.]

[b]New communities are defined as follows:

The goal of "new communities" may be seen as a balanced use of land which encompasses housing, commerce, and industry, through a broad range of housing types, and through higher service standards in community health, education, and social services. [From Margaret E. Goertz, *New Towns in U.S.* (Austin, Tex.: Office of Research, Lyndon B. Johnson School of Public Administration, The University of Texas at Austin, 1973), p. 1.]

1

PUDs are so striking, and the trend is increasingly in that direction, the spillover issue is likely to become more and more significant.

Economic analyses have demonstrated that PUDs offer attractive methods whereby private developers achieve the economies of scale development and reap special advantages from residential-commercial-industrial development within a reasonable time frame.[1] On the public side, the PUDs can be potentially attractive by providing controls over their scale, intensity, design, open space, and public service/tax components.

There appears to be a growing market for various types of PUDs ranging from modified, low-density developments dominated by town-house construction to higher-density developments dominated by garden apartments and occasional high-rise construction. The mix of industrial-commercial uses with residential use can also vary widely. In addition, PUDs are beginning to make inroads into very different but growing housing markets: retirees, empty-nesters, single persons, and young couples, as well as more traditional suburban family units with children, in which the breadwinner chooses to commute long distances to a job for the sake of giving his family what he perceives as a safe and healthful environment.

The conditions militating in favor of PUDs suggest that the movement is likely to grow at an accelerated rate. The reasons for this conclusion include:

1. Rising prices for developable sites, which promote tendencies toward higher-density development on a scale large enough to permit developers to capture collateral benefits from private amenities and services, such as shops and offices.
2. Demographic trends that seem to offer favorable market conditions, trends such as a reduction in family size, increases in the number of unmarried persons, a growing population of aged persons, and generally rising levels of income and education.

Aside from their effect on PUD planning and development, these trends are partly responsible for the enormous shift in housing preferences toward apartment and town-house construction as opposed to the free-standing suburban dwelling. (In 1972 multifamily residential construction in New Jersey outstripped single-family construction;[2] according to building permit data for 1972 calendar year, new construction applications for housing units in multifamily structures totalled 35,937 compared with 29,602 single type family units.) In response to changing tastes, the developers have begun to respond to consumer preferences, which emphasize amenities, as well as high-quality planning and design, and which alleviate anxieties about security and schools, major concerns of core city outmigrants.

At this point, it is useful to define *PUDs* and *new communities*. In this respect, the New Jersey legislation that authorizes the construction of PUDs is not particularly useful since it establishes a minimum standard of "five dwelling units, five commercial units or three industrial uses, singly or in combination."[3] This obviously reaches well down into the category of small subdivisions. In practice, however, the PUDs in the state are large and becoming larger. PUDs are not mere pebbles thrown into the pond, but larger and larger stones, and the ripple effect is substantial. As noted in a recent study, for example, most of the New Jersey PUDs are between 400 and 800 acres in size, that is, almost in the new-community class.[4] Moreover, plans for PUDs since 1972 fall into a smaller new-town category since they range between 1000 and 2500 acres in size.

In addition to the PUDs, a number of full-scale new communities have been proposed for south Jersey and other parts of the state, including a major new development along the Jersey City waterfront—a new-town-in-town. Each of these half-dozen new-town proposals calls for construction of a minimum of 10,000 dwelling units.

By definition, most PUD and new-communities activity has taken place on sizable tracts of open land. Policies are required to ensure that new development in the penumbra area surrounding the planned area is harmonious and complementary or, alternatively, that development is sharply delimited to preserve a zone of open space. An entirely new set of problems is posed by the new-town-in-town, few of which exist anywhere in the nation; a number are in the conception or proposal stage, including one suggested for Jersey City. In the case of the new-town-in-town, development normally occurs in open blighted areas, on newly created sites, or on large acreages previously withheld from the market. These in-town sites usually include former railroad yards, filled or re-used land along waterfronts (as in Jersey City), or obsolete public facilities such as military bases.

There are numerous and complex constraints applicable to building new-towns-in-towns. As far as fringe impact is concerned, the development process must focus largely on the relation of the "new town" to existing surrounding development, with respect to possible upgrading or downgrading, conversions, and demolitions, as well as on anticipated impacts on transportation and service facilities.

The central focus of this study is on state policies and programs designed to ensure that the impact of the growing number of PUDs and new communities on surrounding areas will be beneficial rather than harmful. This focus on the primary role of the state in controlling land use around PUDs and new communities is based on several assumptions, some of which are:

1. In New Jersey, there are existing and inherent weaknesses of county government for undertaking the leadership role in land development.
2. The land adjoining and influenced by PUDs overlaps the boundaries of individual municipalities.
3. Land surrounding PUDs often presents difficult environmental challenges and could therefore meet the criteria for state "critical-areas" responsibilities.

As one authority notes:

Presently, state land-use policy is an aggregate of thousands of unrelated decisions made by single-purpose agencies, local governments and private developers without regard for each other or regional, state and national concerns.

The goal, therefore, should be to evolve and promote development policies and programs, taking into account both people's and nature's needs for the purpose of minimizing the areas of conflict and discovering and enhancing the areas of harmony.[5]

As will be discussed in the text that follows, the existing system of land-use regulation, patterns, and incentives in New Jersey has serious deficiencies, particularly in its overemphasis on traditional instrumentalities, which are linked mainly to the police power. It is also assumed that one of the basic weaknesses in the current system of land-use regulation is the fragmentation of municipal planning and regulatory authority. In practical terms, this means that a sparsely populated community with limited staff and technical capability finds it difficult to meet the enormous problem of responding to the new pressures and problems generated by a very large, new PUD within its borders, let alone the problems of overspill effects. In addition, there is the certainty that adjoining communities, equally limited in technical capability and staff resources, will encounter serious problems in confronting unforeseen but significant consequences generated by the new development in the neighboring municipality.

The problem of planning and regulating developments that affect more than one jurisdiction is underscored by Richard Slavin:

In the last few decades a very large gap has appeared in this land-use control mechanism with respect to multi-jurisdictional issues that do not coincide with city and county boundaries. Decisions of small communities adversely affect the environment, economies and social conditions of entire regions and no way has been found to deal with them effectively. The solution to this problem requires that the State realign its development planning and control mechanisms and those of city and county governments. This realignment appears to require the State to increase its policy-making role and provide higher standards for public agencies' performance.[6]

What complicates the above situation is the fact that conflict and inconsistencies are exacerbated by the absence of clearly-stated state goals and policies relating to urban development. The state planning process has thus far failed to come to grips with issues involving population size and distribution, housing needs and mixes, and the growth and distribution of economic activities. To further complicate the problem, partial state functional and operational plans in transportation and other areas have not been rationally integrated. Moreover, these deficiencies in state planning processes are fully in evidence at the county level. It is clear that the development of a useful state policy for land-use and related development is crucial to the issue of PUD impacts. For example, state policy is needed to control the number, size, distribution, and location of PUDs. An issue critical to New Jersey is the extent to which PUDs will have separate, distinct, and autonomous identities and not be permitted to be part of an amorphous mass of subdivisions, flowing one into the other, as is already the case in much of the state. Furthermore, the state will be required to play a crucial role in sensitive areas that deeply concern central cities and suburbs. This is the extent to which new development will be required to adopt a deliberate affirmative policy to achieve racially and economically balanced communities.

The study presents a number of proposals for new and revised policies and programs:

1. These are based on the premise that early planning for PUD impact areas is required well in advance of actual construction.
2. They assume that state policies and programs must make imaginative use of powers of eminent domain and taxation.
3. The final assumption is that changes in jurisdiction, powers, and techniques for land-use regulation represent only the foundation for effective action.

The extent to which state intervention will be effective also depends on the quality of the staff. Implementation of the recommendations call for the creative, tactful, and energetic application of broad administrative discretion, and people who possess the technical proficiency and personal abilities to implement a program of this nature are all too rare. In practice, state intervention not only requires a legislative framework, but also implies the recruitment and organization of well-trained staff working closely with counties and municipalities, emphasizing incentives rather than punitive regulations and capable of negotiating with public officials and private entrepreneurs.

2 Control of Land Development by Application of Police Power

The control of land development through the application of police power is as old as government itself; the formulation and use of building codes, housing codes, and city planning and zoning can be traced back to ancient civilizations. It has been suggested that the grandfather of modern-day zoning in the United States was the 1916 New York City ordinance that regulated the use and location of buildings throughout the city. In any event, the modern version of land-use regulation dates back to the middle and late 1920s when states began to adopt their own versions of the Standard City Planning Enabling Act and the Standard Zoning Enabling Act drafted by Advisory Committees to the United States Department of Commerce. The nation's larger cities had been actively involved in coping with land-use problems through special legislative acts for some years. In addition there were numerous examples of small, fully or partially planned communities ranging from company towns to "utopian" municipalities to large-scale speculative residential developments of varying quality.

In view of subsequent allegations that zoning represents some sort of radical scheme to deprive private property owners of basic rights, it is interesting to note that encouragement for the planning-zoning movement came from Herbert Hoover, then United States Secretary of Commerce, during the heyday of business-dominated politics—the 1920s—and that the cutting edge of support came from developers and property owners, as well as municipalities. Planning and zoning were regarded as a form of property protection, an essential means for protecting property values for the affluent—that is, those who had significant investments to conserve.

The landmark court decision in zoning was the 1926 *Euclid* v. *Ambler Realty* case, which determined that states have the constitutional power to regulate land use and to delegate this power to their political subdivisions, the municipalities. Once delegated, power is difficult to retrieve and municipalities jealously guard their land-use prerogatives from other municipalities, counties, states, and the federal government.

From the viewpoint of many property owners, traditional plan-ning and zoning practices have worked reasonably well in the past half-century. This attitude of satisfaction is particularly characteris-tic of the so-called "country club suburbs," which have effectively used their land-use control powers to maintain homogeneous, upper-income communities. Planning and zoning have worked less well from the viewpoint of other segments of the population, particu-larly the disadvantaged and racial minorities.

It would be useful at this point to examine some of the assump-tions of traditional land-use control mechanisms to discover why this historically rather staid, legalistic field has recently emerged as an arena of controversial struggle over fundamental social and economic issues. The first assumption is that the community will develop a comprehensive plan guiding its growth, which includes clear directions for land use, and that these directions will subse-quently be embodied in a zoning ordinance and official map consis-tent with the comprehensive plan. It is assumed that once these steps have been taken, land-use control is virtually self-regulating. Related to this assumption is the belief that planning and zoning are professional and technical value-free processes in which the techni-cian assists the community in implementing noncontroversial, con-sensual land-use objectives.

In practice, land-use regulation has proved disappointing, both internally and externally. Within municipalities, there has been a consistent pattern of critical land-use decisions being made piecemeal through variances, zoning amendments, special permits, and exceptions. Justified mainly on the basis of individual owner hardship, these cases have had cumulative effects in achieving fun-damental alterations in the nature of entire neighborhoods. This exception process is the continuing source of tension and confronta-tion between planning and zoning administrators. The shift of decision-making powers in land use to zoning boards of appeal has led to charges in many communities that comprehensive planning is a futile exercise continually undercut by politically oriented laymen.

Externality is even a greater problem in land-use regulation than intramunicipal problems relating to failure to implement com-prehensive plans. As presently constituted, land-use control does not take into account the growing interdependency among municipalities, particularly those in close physical proximity, not only in terms of land use, but in many economic and social areas.

The failure to give adequate consideration in land-use decisions to the impacts on neighboring communities grows out of the competitiveness spawned by struggles to preserve and enhance the local tax base and to safeguard communities against perceived dangers from the intrusions of social and physical problems.

In more recent years, intercommunity competition has grown more sophisticated and more selective. Many communities vie for prestigious corporate headquarters and research facilities, but few manifest interest in heavy industry or discount shopping centers, despite the pressures on local ratables. In addition, most communities have become extremely sensitized to social and environmental problems and display varying degrees of resistance toward new developments which carry the risks of environmental degradations or social frictions. Formerly, it was not only implicitly believed, despite growing evidence to the contrary, that such intercommunity conflicts as are mentioned above, were rare, but it was assumed as well that these few conflicts could be resolved at the county or state level. In practice, the higher-level adjudication process has been generally ineffective. State and regional land-use control powers have been no match for the political bypass mechanisms under which aggrieved municipalities succeed in indefinitely stalling or otherwise overriding state and/or regional mandates.

While this general sketch of land-use regulatory history, approaches, and problems is nationwide in scope, it applies with particular force in the state of New Jersey. This is the case not only because of the state's highly urbanized character, which exacerbates its land-use problems, but also because of the state's extreme jurisdictional fragmentation. (New Jersey contains 567 cities, boroughs, towns, townships, and villages, over half of which have total populations of less than 5000).

Existing Forms of Land-Use Regulation in New Jersey

Reflecting historical comments as to the roots and origins of land-use regulations throughout the country, New Jersey's land-use control methods—municipal planning, municipal official map regulation, municipal zoning and municipal subdivision control—date back to the late 1920s. New Jersey's several enabling acts in land-use regulation have been periodically revised to incorporate newer concepts and approaches. With one exception—the 1967 Municipal Planned Unit Development Act—these enabling acts still exhibit many of the weaknesses that have previously been identified.

New Jersey's planning enabling act contains basic provisions for a planning mechanism with powers that are essential research and advisory in character. Municipal planning boards are permitted —not required—to prepare and adopt master plans covering the physical development of the municipality, including the use of land and building, services, transportation, housing, conservation, public facilities, population distribution and density, historic sites, and so on. Since the master plan is adopted by the planning board, and not by the governing body of the municipality, it does not necessarily represent official public policy. The reason for the gap between the planning board and the governing body can be found in the historical tradition of insulating the planning board from the political process. It was believed that planning was a technical and aesthetic speciality that would inevitably be corrupted if brought under direct control of the currently elected officials. Thus the enabling act provides for overlapping terms of appointed citizens to ensure both insulation and continuity of the planning agency from one municipal administration to the next. In addition to authorization to prepare and adopt a master plan and to make other studies and investigations relating to planning and physical development, planning boards are confined entirely to review-and-comment responsibilities.

New Jersey's zoning enabling act, adopted in 1928,[1] also follows traditional lines. The strengths of its form and substance lie in the predictability and protective classification of districts and uses of land, which result in a reasonable measure of orderly physical development and in the conservation of values for predesignated land parcels. The weaknesses of this traditional approach to zoning include the extreme emphasis that it places on explicit segregation of land uses, which may tend to produce sterile patterns of residential development. Furthermore, it also permits incompatible uses in "lower" districts, for example, residential subdivisions in zones of heavy industry. Another related weakness is the inordinate emphasis on control of single parcels rather than regulation of unified area development.

New Jersey's subdivision control enabling act,[2] incorporated in the municipal planning enabling act, is also framed along traditional lines. Subdivision control provisions require developers to prepare engineering site plans for municipal approval. The site plan must cover such matters as the locations and specifications for streets and sidewalks, drainage, locations of utilities, and possibly the dedication of open space and sites for such public facilities as schools. Although traditional subdivision control is far preferable to parcel-by-parcel development on grounds of efficiency and reduced costs, it still has serious weaknesses. These include relatively limited design control exercised by the municipality. Moreover, the review process is one-shot rather than continuing in scope. In addition, open space, which may be deeded by the developer to the municipality, tends to be fragmented and therefore of limited usefulness. Finally, developers may be required to install expensive utilities overdesigned for their subdivisions and geared to serve future subdivisions linked into utility systems.

The New Jersey Official Map and Building Permit Act, adopted in 1953,[3] is intended to govern and protect the location and width of streets and drainage rights of way, and the reservation and preservation from encroachment of public parks and playgrounds.

Partly as a response to the weaknesses of traditional land-use controls, New Jersey adopted the Municipal Planned Unit Development Act of 1967.[4] Most of the major features of PUD are derived from the existing land-use system of controls. As indicated by one authority on the subject, PUD offers

. . . a program-oriented, mid-range plan, legally binding upon participants. PUD also continues a trend in modern zoning towards flexibility in land use emphasizing a mixture of land uses, unit development, and wide-ranging administrative discretion to local officials. Finally, PUD continues the movement away from preset regulation in subdivision control and fosters new interest in the municipal/developer bargaining process. As a result, it offers the developer a more streamlined platting process and potentially larger profits in exchange for an increase in the municipality's site plan review powers and a procedural mechanism for assembling usable amounts of contiguous open space. PUD goes one step further by offering for the first time land use control that enables a municipality to control effectively both the tempo and sequence of an area's development.[5]

Despite the fact that the PUD represents a major improvement in land-use control enabling legislation, it still contains a number of weaknesses, many of which have already been identified:

1. Failure to require land-use development plans for areas adjacent to but lying outside the perimeters of the PUD.

2. The failure to require coordination with the planning-land-use regulation processes in neighboring municipalities, which may be strongly affected by construction of the PUD.
3. Lack of any assurance that municipal responsibilities and commitments will be effectively exercised.

Moreover, PUD enabling legislation does not of itself require that the municipality and developer give adequate attention to social mix or to environmental impact.

The New Jersey County and Regional Planning Enabling Act[6] was adopted in 1935, during a period of planning activity inspired by the New Deal. The act provides for county and regional planning boards whose powers and duties parallel those of municipal planning boards, that is, their responsibilities are largely research and advisory in character. The county planning board is assigned the responsibility for preparing and adopting a master plan for physical development of the county, for preparing an official county map, for reviewing subdivisions, and for assuming municipal planning powers if the municipality so desires.

All of the land-use control weaknesses identified for municipalities fully apply at the county and/or regional level. In addition, county government in New Jersey has basic shortcomings. As described in a major report prepared by the County and Municipal Government Study Commission, basic deficiencies prevent this level of government from dealing effectively with land-use problems: (1) legal inadequacy; (2) fiscal inadequacy; (3) structural and administrative inadequacy; and (4) political inadequacy.[7] Given these handicaps, it is not surprising that observers feel that, at best, no more than one-third of New Jersey's 20 counties have productive and useful planning agencies.

Hackensack Meadows, located close to New York City, has long been considered an area ripe for physical development. One of the obstacles in exploiting this overlooked potential was the fact that the Meadows sprawled across a number of political jurisdictions. To meet this challenge, the state adopted the Hackensack Meadowland Reclamation and Development Act in 1968.[8] As provided by the act, a separate commission was established to guide the development of approximately 21,000 acres of marshland located in 14 different municipalities and two counties. In scale and concept, at least, the legislation represented authorization for state intervention to assist in the creation of model developments, such as new communities.

In terms of its scale, the Hackensack Meadowlands legislation covers an area far larger than any existing or planned PUDs in New Jersey and far larger in scale than most new towns, which rarely cover an area greater than 10,000 acres. By its very nature, the Hackensack Meadowlands is subject to very sensitive ecological issues, especially those relating to drainage. Moreover, the Meadowlands is an open area in the midst of densely developed areas of New Jersey and its development therefore requires careful integration with surrounding transportation and other public systems.

There have been a number of complications in the negotiating process for the Meadowlands development, including controversies over densities and over the proposed mix of land uses. In contrast to the typical PUD development, in which bargaining is typically limited to representatives of a municipality and a developer, operations at the scale of Hackensack Meadowlands and new towns generally involve intricate political and technical discussions at the state, and frequently federal, level. Also, because the scale is so large, more than one developer may be required. For this reason, there are extremely complex problems in drawing up proper legal instruments, in drafting adequate sequential plans, in staging and implementing actual construction, in securing a continual flow of sufficient funding, and in marketing the final product. As a result, the process is extremely slow and demands "patient" money, which can wait for returns on investment.

In contrast to traditional American attitudes concerning the location of development, greater attention is now being paid to the environmental setting and ecological consequences than was the case in earlier generations. For many years, marsh lands, coastal plains, flood-prone areas, steep slopes, aquifer recharging areas, and forest lands were considered suitable targets for development, if market conditions were favorable. It was implicitly assumed that man conquers and/or manipulates nature as he pleases, and that ecological consequences could be dealt with through the application of technology, for example, by constructing dams to protect flood-prone areas. In practice, wisdom has been late in coming, but the high cost and futility of coping with unanticipated consequences of heedless development has caused basic changes in public attitudes. One result of this attitudinal shift has been the identification of "critical" target areas requiring governmental protection. In New Jersey, in addition to active state policy on the acquisition and preservation of open space and forest lands, considerable attention has been given in recent years to wetlands, flood-prone areas, coastal plains, and other selective environmental problems. Following the Massachusetts precedent, New Jersey enacted legislation in 1970 designed to protect coastal wetlands.[9] Under this legislation, the State Commissioner of Environmental Protection is empowered to regulate the dredging, filling, removing, or otherwise altering or polluting coastal wetlands, through the establishment of a permit system applicable to such activities.

New Jersey has taken active steps to protect its flood-prone areas by restricting their development and use. The Flood Plains Act of 1972[10] authorized the State Department of Environmental Protection to regulate the development and use of land designated as "floodways," and gave municipalities one year to adopt regulations consistent with state standards relating to "flood fringe areas." The legislation defines "floodways" as "the channel of a natural stream and portions of the flood plain adjoining the channel, which are reasonably required to carry and discharge the flood water or flood flow of any natural stream." It defines "flood fringe area" as that portion of the relatively flat area adjoining the channel of a natural stream which has or may be covered by flood water. The state agency may regulate the development of "flood fringe areas" if a municipality fails to act.

There are two major objectives in the flood plains legislation: (1) to reduce losses from floods; (2) to prevent floods. The legislation seeks to minimize flood losses by prohibiting construction in flood-prone areas and by protecting home purchasers from being tempted to buy from developers building on relatively cheap, flood-prone land. By restricting the intensity of development, the legislation also seeks to prevent flooding.

The constitutional validity of flood plains zoning "is still in doubt because of the paucity of judicial decisions on this issue."[11] However, several court decisions in 1972 in other states have upheld the protection of wetlands, an issue similar to flood plains protection, by prohibiting their draining, filling, and dredging, although such restriction prevented owners from developing their lands. This new trend toward judicial support for ecological concerns and thus against property rights possibly indicates that prohibitions against land development can incorporate flood-risk considerations, despite the 1963 devision of the New Jersey Supreme Court, which held a zoning ordinance invalid for restricting the use of land for flood-water detention purposes.[12]

Alternative Forms of Land-Use Regulation Under Police Power

During the last 20 years, particularly within the past decade, a variety of attempts have been initiated to modernize through modification traditional land-use regulation techniques, in order to make them more responsive to changing physical, economic, and social needs. The principal modifications include the adoption of time controls on land use, the creation of floating zones, contract zoning, incentive zoning, performance zoning, and open space zoning. In the early 1970s, there was a distinct departure from past practice; that is, there was an emergence of environmental impact controls governing most types of major development, as well as the creation of means for the preservation and expansion of open space and natural processes (surface water, marshes, aquifers, flood plains, forests and woodlands, and steep slopes).[13]

Constitutional Limitations on Land-Use Controls

Before proceeding to a systematic discussion of alternative forms of land-use regulation under the police power, a discussion (and understanding) of the principle of constitutional limitations on all forms of land-use control is valuable. Under this principle, zoning, subdivision control, and official map regulations must meet the constitutional test of "reasonableness." Many of the landmark court cases dealing with constitutional limitations of land-development regulations have emerged in states like New Jersey, which have been subjected to particularly pressing problems of suburbanization and urban sprawl. These cases usually involve tests of municipal land-use ordinances adopted by communities located directly in the path of suburbanization and represent attempts to limit, control, and regulate proposed new development.

Three important cases in New Jersey uphold the principle of "reasonableness" in the three major land-use categories of zoning, subdivision control, and the official map—(1) zoning (*Morris*

County Land Improvement Co. v. *Parsippanny-Troy Hills Township*, 1963); (2) subdivision control (*Lake Intervale Homes, Inc.* v. *Parsippanny-Troy Hills Township*, 1958); and (3) official map (*Lomarch Corp.* v. *Mayor of Englewood*, 1968).

The zoning case concerned the constitutional validity of a township zoning ordinance that contained provisions restricting the use of swampland. The New Jersey Supreme Court held in 1963 that this ordinance constituted a taking of land for public purpose without just compensation, and was therefore unconstitutional.

Provisions of the zoning ordinance were designed to impose severe restrictions on the use of swampland in order to retain the land substantially in its natural wetland state as a flood-water detention basin and as a wildlife sanctuary. According to the court opinion, the zoning ordinance was so restricted that the land could not be practically used for any reasonable purpose, including those permitted under the ordinance. Thus these provisions of the zoning ordinance were declared to be confiscatory, beyond delegated police power and statutory authorization.[14]

A similar test of the "reasonableness" of existing land-use regulation in New Jersey concerned subdivision control. This case involved an action against the township of Parsippany-Troy Hills by a developer to recover costs incurred by him for installing water mains required to service his development. The Supreme Court held that application of the ordinance to the developer was clearly arbitrary and discriminatory. The court pointed out that the subdivision regulation ordinance was completely devoid of standards relating to the imposition of costs for the extension of water mains and resulted in the imposition of the total cost on every subdivider without regard to the actual benefits he derived from the improvement. In this case, the developer operated on a relatively small scale and some of his building lots were scattered in isolated pairs throughout the tract. For this reason, water main extensions were necessary along an entire street to service one house in the block. In consequence, other property owners contiguous to the developer's property and abutting on the water main extensions paid for by the developer would benefit therefrom.[15]

With respect to Official Map regulations, in 1968 the New Jersey Supreme Court again came down on the side of "reasonableness" as a constitutional limitation on land-use regulation. In requiring that just compensation must be paid to a property for a temporary reservation of land for future open space purposes, the court upheld the constitutionality of the Official Map legislation but insisted upon just compensation, although the act did not expressly provide therefor.[16]

It can be assumed that the test of "reasonableness," including just compensation for affected property owners, will remain relatively unchallenged as a guiding principle in land-use regulation. If this assumption can be accepted as valid, then the burden of drafting and implementing legislation that applies alternative forms of land-use regulation becomes all the more difficult because the newer devices invariably open up wide areas of administrative discretion in contrast to the more rigid specificity of traditional Euclidian zoning and related land-use controls. In practice, it should be noted, new land-use regulatory devices have opened up interface areas for planning and Law, among other professions, where intricate legal and technical argumentations are presented to the courts for review and adjudication.[17]

Controlled Sequential Development

During the 1960s and early 1970s, courts in several states subjected to major suburbanizations pressures began to take strict anti-exclusionary positions. Under traditional Euclidian principles, communities had been free to adopt large lot requirements and substantial requirements for minimum floor space. They were also free to exclude completely the construction of multifamily dwellings. In effect, this zoned out the poor from large segments of metropolitan areas. In striking down exclusionary zoning, the courts ruled that providing housing for all income classes is a metropolitan responsibility, one that cannot be shirked by component communities employing exclusionary devices. In a landmark 1972 case, however, the New York Court of Appeals upheld the validity of a municipal plan that was designed for carefully phased development. The pace and scale of new construction was to be linked to the availability of essential services and facilities required by the increased population. This device for controlled sequential development was acceptable to the court becasue it was neutral in character, that is, it did not discriminate against the poor and was part of an officially adopted long-term capital improvement program committing the community to further growth. Moreover, developers desiring to accelerate the pace of construction were at liberty to do so by providing the essential service infrastructure themselves.[18]

In discussing the implications of court decisions upholding controlled sequential development, Thomas O'Keefe emphasizes the compatibility of this device in protecting the interests of existing residents while accepting newcomers into the community. (It should be noted that the class, race, or other specification of these newcomers is nowhere explicit or implicit, merely that an orderly influx will be acceptable.)

An initial significant distinction between time controls and other zoning devices that have been voided on exclusionary grounds is that when the time control device is linked with a bona fide comprehensive plan and a formula for gradually including low- and moderate-income housing, the whole scheme takes on an equitable, quasiregional, judicially palatable character. Time controls evidence a spirit of bona fide regulation, not outright exclusion. . . . Time controls regulate but do not freeze growth, and they are flexible enough to accommodate a variety of densities and housing types.[19]

The use of this technique as a means of ensuring high-quality development is also underscored by O'Keefe, who points out that time controls on land use offer a flexible, responsive device for dealing with unpredictable problems.

By phasing growth and the provision of quality municipal services, community residents are instituting a kind of built-in community "quality control" system. This judicious and efficient use of the land redounds to the benefit of outsiders and insiders alike. . . .

To be sure, the controlled growth approach does not solve all the pressing problems of suburban growth clamoring for community attention and dollars. Nor is there a guarantee that gearing development of the capacity of the land to support it will successfully lie ahead. The great strength of time controls is that they deal with the future as it appears now while retaining enough flexibility to adjust to a different world view should the need arise.[20]

The controlled sequential development approach represents a compromise between those communities committed explicitly or implicitly to a growth policy and those communities whose number is ever-increasing which have taken a stand in favor of little or no population expansion. Closely linked to the philosophy of the ecological-environmental movement, some no-growth communities have expressed their opposition to all types of new development by acquisition of inordinate tracts of developable land for open space, and many more have deliberately failed to provide the infrastructure required for urban development. This posture, which is beginning to be adopted by a few states, notably Oregon, Vermont, and Colorado, make this a basic land-use issue at the national level.[21]

Controlled sequential development has been criticized as a potentially dangerous device by which suburban communities may prevent growth and development and discourage the movement of population into the area. This danger was dealt with specifically in the *Ramapo* decision,[22] where the court found that the Ramapo, New York, program was not designed "to freeze population at present levels, but to maximize growth by the efficient use of land, and in so doing testify to this community's continuing role in population assimilation. In sum, Ramapo asks not that it be left alone, but only that it be allowed to prevent the kind of deterioration that has transformed well-ordered and thriving residential communities into blighted ghettos with attendant hazards to health, security, and social stability—a danger not without substantial basis in fact."[23]

In spite of the judicial declaration of purpose on which the validity of this device was sustained, many students of planning law and organizations concerned about the social implications of development timing controls have expressed reservations and apprehensions about the potential misuse of the device to impair the freedom of movement or residence of those outside the municipal borders.[24] For example, a study by the Potomac Institute, Inc. suggests that a given program of controlled sequential development may be invalid for any one of a number of reasons:[25]

1. *Violation of the "due process" clause.* This argument is based upon the premise that the landowner will be deprived of the reasonable use of his property.
2. *Outside the scope of the police power.* This argument is based upon the premise that the "general welfare" requirement upon which all police power regulations are based prevents a locality from ignoring regional housing needs.
3. *Outside the power delegated in the enabling legislation.* This argument is based upon the premise that the zoning powers delegated to municipalities by the state do not include the authority to exclude people from the jurisdiction.

4. *Violation of the "equal protection" clause.* This argument is based upon the premise that exclusionary land-use laws tend to have the greatest impact upon racial minorities.
5. *Violation of the "right to travel."* This argument is based upon the premise that the constitutionally protected right to travel may not be restricted by a municipality's land-use regulations.

To determine whether a given program of controlled sequential development is in fact being used as a device to discourage population movement, the Potomac Institute study suggests, *inter alia*, the following criteria[26]:

1. Is the program responsive to regional housing needs?
2. Does the program provide for housing for employee households with existing or anticipated jobs in the jurisdiction?
3. Does the program contain a real and sincere commitment for public investment to assimilate growth?
4. Does the program apply only to residential development or is the commercial and industrial development coordinated with residential growth?
5. Does the program result in a tax effort that is reduced below the average for the metropolitan area?

On the basis of these and other criteria the study concludes that the device of controlled sequential development was badly applied in Ramapo but that it could, if properly used, become a device for "a more equitable and environmentally sensitive management of urban growth."

Floating Zones

In the late 1940s, a new concept in land-use regulation, known as the "floating zone," began to be applied. This approach is based on the assumptions that the optimum time and/or location for specific land uses cannot always be determined in advance. Its application is generally limited to shopping centers, light industrial and research parks, and garden apartments. This unusual degree of market-responsive location in floating zones is directly opposed to Euclidean zoning, which clearly delineates land-use districts by use, height, and area.

Initially, the floating zone concept was upheld in a 1951 court case in New York state on the grounds that the failure of the municipal zoning ordinance amendment to establish Euclidean boundaries or to make proper changes in the zoning map were not sufficient reason for declaring the ordinance invalid. Like most floating zone ordinances, the zoning ordinance amendments adopted by the village of Tarrytown in 1947 contained clearly defined performance standards on acreage, setbacks, spacing of buildings, and minimum lot size.[27] In Maryland, the Supreme Court upheld the floating zone provisions in a Baltimore County zoning plan, which limited its floating zone provisions to light industry.[28]

In New Jersey, the floating zone technique was declared invalid in 1957 on the grounds that it constituted "spot zoning." Spot zoning is a pejorative term connoting special favors granted to selective owners of individual parcels within a general land-use category. In the New Jersey case, the township of Chesterfield had zoned its entire community into a single district for agricultural and residential uses, with numerous exceptions for business and industrial uses governed by special permits to be granted by the planning board. The court attacked the validity of this ordinance because the state's enabling zoning act, in the court's opinion, required the establishment of territorial use districts based on the character of the land in accordance with Euclidean zoning principles. In addition, the court ruled that the floating zone was contrary to one of the essential purposes of zoning, that is, stabilizing property uses so as to protect existing investments made on the assumption that established use districts are of permanent character.[29]

At this point in time, the courts are still reluctant to depart completely from traditional zoning principles, partly because of the danger that administrative discretion may be abused.

Unmapped zoning, like many of the newer, more flexible zoning techniques, is far more subject to abuse than conventional zoning. Too often they are used as a means of extorting concessions from developers that could not be demanded legally. They may also be an excuse for unsound planning or no planning at all. Before such techniques are used, they must be preceded by specific policies, standards, and regulations designed to inform developers of what the community desires and to protect surrounding land uses. Then, and only then, is a community justified in using the more flexible techniques.[30]

Despite its unfavorable connotations, when spot zoning is

viewed as careful rezoning of small areas, it has, on occasion, been upheld by the courts, usually when its need is demonstrated on the basis of one or more of the following criteria:

(1) The area is to be rezoned for a service business in a residential neighborhood under circumstances indicating a real need for the service.

(2) The existing zone classification has resulted in the complete loss of value of the land to the owner.

(3) The area is located near other rezoned small areas in the same use district or is located in close proximity to other less restrictive use zones.

(4) The area will be used by a public utility to provide areawide service.

(5) The area is significantly affected by increased traffic or is located on existing transportation facilities.

(6) Rezoning of the area will have a demonstrably favorable impact on tax revenues and other economic goals of community-wide interest.[31]

Contract Zoning

The practice of contract zoning typically involves the rezoning of property to a zoning classification with fewer restrictions based on an agreement as to certain conditions between the property owner and the local legislative body. There is a decided split in state judicial opinion as to the legality of this zoning technique. The highest state courts in New Jersey, Florida, and Maryland have ruled contract zoning unlawful; in New York and Massachusetts, on the other hand, the courts have supported the validity of this zoning device. According to a leading authority in zoning:

The general conclusion is that the arguments made by the courts do not warrant an outright condemnation of contract zoning. Its use in certain situations might be quite acceptable.[32]

San Francisco approved a city planning code in 1968 that contains provision for "development bonuses." Developers may be permitted to go beyond floor-area ratio limitations if, for example, the site plan provides for direct access or proximity to a rapid transit system, substantial parking facilities, multiple building entrances, sidewalk widening by means of an arcade, plaza, or other facility, or an observation deck.[33]

Incentive Zoning

"Incentive" or "bonus" zoning establishes arrangements whereby developers who meet certain special conditions are permitted to reap higher profits, usually from more intensive development of their projects. In return for building in certain areas, for constructing certain kinds of buildings, for adding parking spaces or public amenities, developers are usually allowed to increase their floor-area ratios. The bonus device is particularly applicable to densely-settled core areas in which developers propose to construct high-rise buildings.

Although incentive zoning has not yet been tested in the courts, one authority believes that it will be upheld if planners make careful use of the instrument.

Although some courts might experience difficulty in overcoming the apparent lack of explicit statutory authorization for incentive zoning, the likelihood that it will receive judicial approval remains great. . . . As long as the planners go into court armed with well-documented, comprehensive studies to back up their plans, it is doubtful that the courts will view an incentive zoning case as the occasion to reverse the prior trend of judicial approval.[34]

Performance Zoning

Performance zoning, usually focused on industrial land use, represents an attempt to apply output measures to specific types of development as a substitute for generic types of classification found in most zoning ordinances. Traditional zoning classification generally separates manufacturing into light and heavy industrial zones although there is recognition of the fact that some types of industrial activities classified as "heavy" generate fewer harmful impacts on the environment than some so-called light industries.

A good example of how performance standards can be incorporated into a local zoning ordinance may be found in the proposed zoning ordinance for Rome, New York.[35] These zoning provisions required applicants for building permits in manufacturing zoning districts to submit sworn statements that the proposed uses would be operated in accordance with stipulated performance standards governing noise or vibration; fire, explosive, or other hazards; smoke, dust, dirt, or other forms of air pollution; electrical or other disturbances; glare; or other factors adversely affecting the surrounding area. The ordinance also provided for continued compliance through the activities of an enforcement officer.

While performance zoning appears to be a major advance in encouraging greater flexibility through increased precision in a manner similar to performance-type building codes, in practice the administration of performance standards even in the limited field of industrial zoning has proved to be extraordinarily complex and difficult.

After an initial surge of enthusiasm about the concept, some lawyers and planners seem to have had second thoughts. Although many municipalities have adopted standards in some form, their enforcement too often has been turned over to administrative machinery which, in Norman Williams' pungent phrase, "can't keep track of a copy of the current zoning map." On the other hand, in a few cases, such as that of New Haven, their adoption was based on an optimistic but probably reasonable estimate of future capabilities.[36]

Specific technical problems that have arisen, particularly in enforcement of zoning performance standards, include:

1. The shortage of qualified technicians to administer standards, a deficiency that represents a continuing obstacle to their wider use.
2. The unresolved issue of whether standards for pollution emissions should vary from one district to another.
3. The question of how far performance standards should be extended to bring together land uses now considered incompatible.

Open Space Zoning

Zoning has been relied upon as a major technique for providing open space to an urbanizing population. Although the creation of open space through zoning was never intended to be a complete substitute for the acquisition and development of public open space (parks, public reservations forest reserves, beaches, wilderness sites, and so on), under eminent domain and purchase, both zoning and subdivision control have produced considerable amounts of open space, albeit of a limited character and benefit.

The issue of open space zoning raises serious and difficult constitutional and legal problems, many of which have not been resolved in the courts. As a general rule, courts have been solicitous of the individual rights of the property owner. By preventing or restricting development, open space zoning tends to detract from the value of an immediately affected property. While in some cases, the preservation of a given tract of open space can be converted into measurable benefits for adjoining and nearby residents, in many instances, the benefits of open space inure to the public at large—for example, in the case of a forest preserve or a beach. There are no clear-cut judicial tests to determine whether open space provisions, which preclude payment of just compensation, are constitutionally valid. While the courts have traditionally been receptive to open space zoning arguments based on public safety and prevention of nuisances, there is far less judicial precedent and support for regulation of private land use to achieve aesthetic objectives. Judicial doubts are due to the elusive nature of aesthetic definition and to the fact that, unlike public safety and welfare, such amenities appear to be "luxury and indulgence" rather than "necessity."[37]

There are three principal approaches to generating open space through zoning. Under the first approach, zoning is designed simply to forbid development, thereby reserving the designated area as open space. The principal deficiency with this approach is the general finding by the courts that this represents an invalid infringement on the rights of the property owner. In one New Jersey case, for example, the court held invalid an ordinance that rezoned a tract of land for park and school use that the borough had previously unsuccessfully attempted to purchase. "The court found that although the land was well suited to park and school purposes the ordinance was so restrictive as to amount to a taking without compensation."[38]

The more common technique for adding open space through zoning is under the bulk, height, and minimum lot provisions of zoning ordinances. In residential areas, this results in the allocation of space to side yards, lawns, and rear yards, which make varying amounts of open space available to residents. A variation of this approach is the incentive zoning provision, which extends to developers the option of building more intensively on sites in exchange for constructing plazas and other open areas. This technique is most applicable to densely built-up areas, where plazas and arcades are found adjacent to office buildings. While this is an improvement over traditional practice, which made no provision at all for open areas in high-rise developments, there is some question as to whether the public benefit from this trade-off is sufficient. The open spaces provided under these arrangements are often unusable and minimal, and frequently they offer poor compensation for the added height and bulk of the buildings which may increase population density unreasonably and block off light and air.

Incentive zoning could be strengthened by improving the trade-off: the approval of higher floor-area ratios should be carefully weighed against the quality and usability of the proposed open spaces.

One of the more controversial approaches to providing open space through zoning is by requiring substantial minimum lots for housing. The traditional "country-club" suburb may incorporate minimum lot provisions ranging from one to five acres. This technique has certain direct benefits to residents, most of whom, by definition, are affluent. It prevents the intrusion of low-income families and preserves a visually attractive "green" community. It also reserves sufficient land around each home for the construction of extensive and varied recreation facilities, which may include tennis courts, paddocks, swimming pools, greenhouses, and formal gardens.

The courts have tended to validate minimum lot zoning as appropriate for semirural communities and "superior" residential districts. In a New Jersey case, the court upheld a five-acre minimum lot requirement as an appropriate means of preserving the rural character of a community and maintaining property values.[39] In a Virginia case, however, the court declared a similar zoning ordinance invalid. The county had zoned its larger western two-thirds for two-acre minimum lots to channel a tide of growth flowing out of Washington, D.C. into the already developed eastern portion of the county. The ordinance was struck down on the grounds that it prevented lower-income groups from moving into the area.[40]

The opinion of the Virginia court has been echoed in other states, including New Jersey.[41] More recent judicial decisions indicate that the courts do not view the real or perceived harm accruing to residents of large-lot communities as sufficient grounds for effectively barring the entrance of low- and middle-income families. The courts are underscoring the fact that such communities are part of a larger metropolitan community and can therefore be reasonably expected to assume part of the responsibility for providing building sites for low- and middle-income families and open space for residents of a larger segment of the metropolitan area than reside within the community's boundaries.

In addition to traditional zoning, subdivision control has also been used to create open space. The primary method under subdivision control is through the dedication by the developer of stated amounts of open land as a condition for plat approval. Although the courts have upheld this subdivision requirement when the benefits are clearly reserved for residents of the subdivision,[42] when the benefits of open space are more general in nature, the municipality rather than the developer must bear the cost.[43]

There are several disadvantages to providing open space through dedication under subdivision control:

1. Not every subdivision has land suitable for park development.
2. Many subdivisions are too small to provide enough land for open space utilization.
3. Leaving the provision of open space to developer initiative is incompatible with sound comprehensive planning.

A second method of utilizing subdivision control to generate open space is through the imposition of fees on the subdivision developer in lieu of dedication. Under this technique, the community can pool the fee contributions from a number of developers, thereby providing greater flexibility in the choice and development of public open space. The difficulty here is to ensure that the fees and benefits are directly related to the developer's activities. For example, in a California case, the collection of fees for a city-wide park fund was disapproved on the ground that the subdivider was being charged with improvements that his development had not necessitated.[44]

A more recent approach to open space under zoning and subdivision control is through cluster zoning, contract zoning, or planned unit development. Under these arrangements, the developer agrees to group structures so as to leave substantial areas for common space. Representing major improvements over past practices in which inadequate provision is made for public open areas, these techniques are limited in that they reserve such open spaces to residents alone. Cluster zoning has the special advantages of reducing the cost of providing municipal facilities and services, for example, water and sewers, while at the same time providing substantial amounts of accessible open space at no cost to the municipality.

A *Harvard Law Review* article concludes that the potential for open space preservation under the police power is limited. It emphasizes (1) that open space created under this largely piecemeal approach is not likely to be consistent with a comprehensive plan for municipal open space; and (2) that such small scale, *ad hoc* open space development does not contribute significantly to achieving regional goals for open space and other regional objectives.[45]

Environmental Impact Control

Beginning roughly in the 1950s and gathering momentum in the subsequent decade, there has been a broadening sentiment for increased attention to the environment and the general quality of life. Initially, the response to this concern was compartmentalized, focusing separately on such issues as air pollution, water pollution, the "pesticide peril," noise pollution, solid waste disposal, and overpopulation. The early 1970s saw a gathering of the separate threads into an organized framework, the principal expression of which is the "environmental impact statement." The environmental impact statement and the movement of which it is a part represent an additional stage in the maturation of views toward the concept of land and its uses. Traditional land-use regulation assumed that land was a commodity and court decisions tended to focus on the rights of the property owner and the preservation and enhancement of property values. Newer concepts of land, which emerged in connection with such issues as "snob zoning" cases, as well as environmental law, center on broader societal goals and values. The environmental impact statement is a technical brief that is prepared to substantiate that a proposed development is not environmentally harmful.

The National Environmental Policy Act of 1969[46] required federal agencies, or other agencies using federal funds for projects that significantly affect the quality of the human environment, to prepare a statement incorporating five major components:

1. The environmental impact of the proposed action.
2. Any unavoidable adverse environmental effects that might arise should the proposal be implemented.

3. Alternatives to the proposed action.
4. The relationship between short-term uses of man's environment and the maintenance and enhancement of long-term productivity.
5. Any irreversible and irretrievable commitments of resources that would be involved in the proposed action should it be implemented.[47]

The concept of the environmental impact statement has been adopted and applied to private development. California, for example, enacted legislation in 1971 requiring state agencies to prepare environmental impact statements similar to those required of federal agencies.[48] More important, the state of California subsequently adopted legislation under which local authorities can approve or disapprove private developments based on environmental criteria. Projects can be disapproved if they are found likely "to cause substantial environmental damage" or "serious public health problems." A "land project" is defined as a subdivision containing 50 or more parcels. The most recent California amendment to this legislation, effective December 4, 1972, makes it necessary that basic environmental impact questions be asked in virtually every "discretionary act" of local government, including zoning, tentative and final official map approvals, and building permits. Roberts summarizes the current California pattern as follows:

All land use decisions which may affect the quality of the environment in California are now covered by some form of EIS (environmental impact statement). . . . Furthermore, since California has adopted such a statewide policy, it is very likely that many other states will develop their own similar or related programs.[49]

In general, this new environmental emphasis constitutes a necessary reform in a relatively neglected area. It does raise, however, difficult technical, legal, political, and economic issues, which may take years to resolve. For example, there are serious deficiencies in the state-of-the-art that hinder the establishment of defensible environmental standards. The single and synergistic effects of many types of pollutants are still unknown. Until technically unassailable standards can be developed, the courts lack sufficient guidelines for decisions concerning what represents "substantial damage" or "serious problems." There is also the danger that environmental arguments may be used as a smokescreen or surrogate to mask other concerns. A number of affluent communities, for example, have blocked the construction of low- and middle-income housing developments on the basis of their alleged harmful environmental impacts. Often an environmental impact issue involving economic development pits relatively affluent groups with secure assets and incomes against upwardly mobile blue-collar workers, who are primarily interested in jobs and much less concerned with open space and related environmental benefits.

An important and neglected side effect of imposing difficult and complex environmental standards is the tendency to discriminate against smaller developers who cannot afford to finance expensive environmental analyses. This can result in the freezing out of small firms in favor of larger corporations with substantial resources who can bear both the added costs and the significant delays entailed by elaborate environmental studies.

3

Control of Land Development Through Use of Eminent Domain

The previous chapter of this report focused on the use of police power to regulate land in the public interest. An equally important legal tool for controlling land-use development is eminent domain—the power to acquire land needed for public purposes upon payment of reasonable compensation to the owner. While eminent domain is routinely used by state and local government to purchase sites for parks, schools, highways, and so on, it is rarely used to acquire sizable tracts for large-scale public or private development. In the United States, the two principal exceptions to this observation have been (1) the urban renewal program, under which substantial areas were taken under eminent domain in blighted urban areas for subsequent planned re-use; and (2) the open space acquisition program, under which most acreage has been acquired in suburban and rural areas. The impetus for both of these major uses of eminent domain powers emanates from the federal government, which provides the lion's share of necessary funds for land acquisition.

There are several practical problems in any large-scale use of eminent domain. The first is the high cost of purchase. Juries in eminent domain cases tend to be generous toward affected property owners, and eminent domain proceedings leave considerable room for maneuver for persons with political influence or inside knowledge. The second problem is the resistance of the local community because of fear that substantial public land purchases will further erode the municipal tax base. A corollary fear of some competing property owners is that large amounts of public land will be "dumped" on the market, thereby depressing local land values.

Constitutional Issues

From a legal standpoint, the use of eminent domain raises a critical constitutional issue—that acquisition must be for a "public use."[1] Related to this issue is whether land acquired for future public use

31

can be leased in the interim to a private person.[a,2] These basic issues have been satisfactorily resolved by the courts in favor of the principle of eminent domain. Moreover, mainly under the influence of urban renewal, the courts have given "public use" greater flexibility, including the sale of publicly condemned property to private persons for private development under an approved renewal plan.[3] Despite some narrow judicial interpretations of the term "public use," "the modern view is that the Constitution requires only that a 'public benefit' must result from the taking."[4]

The remainder of this chapter is divided into two major segments: (1) a summary of the relatively limited and traditional approaches to eminent domain used in the state of New Jersey, and (2) a description and analysis of innovative techniques in use in other states and abroad, techniques that suggest ways in which New Jersey may make more effective use of its eminent domain powers to achieve land-development objectives.

Use of Eminent Domain in New Jersey

New Jersey laws authorize state and municipal agencies to use the power of eminent domain in five principal categories of development-related policy:

1. Acquisition of sites for public buildings and transportation facilities.
2. Acquisition of open space, parks, and playgrounds.
3. Acquisition for achieving a variety of conservation and recreation purposes.
4. Acquisition for flood control projects.
5. Acquisition under the state's urban redevelopment statutes.

Public agencies using eminent domain power are required to institute condemnation proceedings under separate legal provisions dealing with compensation awards and related matters.[5]

Municipalities, for example, are specifically empowered to use

---

[a]In *City and County of Honolulu* v. *Bishop Trust Company,* the court held that the rental of a building taken by eminent domain for future use as a park represented a temporary and necessary exercise of care to maintain the property until the public use was accomplished. However, it is not clear whether the courts would approve leases to private individuals over long interim periods even if the ultimate uses were public.

eminent domain in addition to other acquisition devices for acquiring open space and related facilities, such as public parks, playgrounds, beaches, water fronts, places for public resort and recreation, lakes and ponds, and so on.[6]

As for acquisitions for conservation purposes and to obtain regional park areas, although New Jersey long had used eminent domain powers to accomplish these purposes, not until the past decade was extensive use made of this legal instrument. The Green Acres Land Acquisition Act of 1961[7] (under which New Jersey had acquired approximately 100,000 acres during the 1961-1971 period from a bond fund of 61 million dollars) and Title VII of the Housing Act of 1961 were the catalysts for large-scale acquisition of land tracts for conservation, park, open space, and recreation purposes. New Jersey's 1961 Green Acres Act authorized state acquisition of lands for these purposes and provided matching grants of up to 50 percent of local acquisition costs to political subdivisions in the state. Moreover, this statute, unlike those of more states, also authorized state acquisitions and approved grants to municipal governments to be used for lands subject to development rights and conservation easements, thereby permitting the acquisition of interests in open space at less than fee, a technique that is less expensive than fee simple acquisition. An additional advantage of this alternative technique is that it keeps the land on the tax rolls.

The evident popularity of this initial legislation to encourage the acquisition of open space for recreation and conservation purposes prompted a second authorization under the New Jersey Green Acres Land Acquisition Act of 1971, approved early in 1972, which was similar in objectives and scope to earlier legislation of 1971 and 1972. The legislature appropriated $72 million from an approved $80 million Green Acres Bond Act of 1971. The 1972 legislation also required special attention to be focused on the most critical need for open lands, in the state's urban areas. As in the prior legislation, half the funds were allocated to lands to be owned by the state, and the other half to cover grants to local governments equal to a maximum of 50 percent of the actual cost of acquired lands. Finally, the act continued the authorization of the earlier legislation to use the open space acquisition funds for lands subject to development rights and conservation easements.[8]

New Jersey statutes also authorize the use of eminent domain powers for flood control projects, including the acquisition of property in the beds of streams, lakes, streets, highways, and rights-of-way.[9]

Finally, an important step forward in the extension of eminent domain power is its authorization under New Jersey's urban redevelopment law. Municipalities may acquire property under this statute by purchase or condemnation proceedings. Under the federal urban renewal program, municipalities may then reconvey such land to private redevelopers.[10]

Eminent Domain: Innovative Techniques

Advance Land Acquisition

The eminent domain power may be used to acquire land in advance for future public use. The future use of such land need not be as precisely detailed as in the case of an urban renewal plan. Advance acquisition provides an opportunity to acquire land before adjacent development or improvements increase its market value. Moreover, with the greater lead time permitted by advance land acquisition, public improvements can be better planned and scheduled, and private developers can program their activities on a long-term basis.

Although advance land acquisition is considered an innovative approach to land policy, there are deep historic roots for the use of large-scale public acquisition to achieve broad development objectives. The classic example is the acquisition of lands in the Northwest Territory and beyond by purchase, treaty, or other means, and the subsequent opening up of these territories for agricultural settlement, pasturage, railroad construction, and canal building by means of no-cost or low-cost transfer of lands to individuals or corporations for various developmental purposes. In a real sense, the nation, from its very beginnings, has pursued advance land acquisition for a public benefit on an enormous scale.

Public land acquisition has also long been used for planned urbanization. While the best known example is Washington, D.C., there are numerous other experiences ranging from military base communities to government installations like Oak Ridge, Tennessee, the Greenbelt communities of the 1930s, and the urban renewal program of the 1950s and 1960s. More recently, the tradition of special public subsidy for new community development has reappeared through Title VII of the National Housing and Urban Development Act of 1968. In addition, there is a tradition of disposing of obsolete federal installations by transferring them to state and local government.

There is an equally long historic tradition in the use of advance land acquisition for public open space. Large proportions of the western states and Alaska were acquired early and have remained in public ownership. Many states and municipalities followed federal precedent by acquiring wilderness areas or farm land close to urban centers for various types of open space uses. The New Jersey Green Acres program and the federal Open Space program are more recent examples of public open space acquisition.

The critical issue in early land acquisition is not the taking or purchase of wilderness areas designated for retention in their natural state. The primary problem in highly urbanized states, such as New Jersey, relates to the control and quality of existing and future urban development. Specifically, the main issue is how best to guide, through a combination of public acquisition and private action, the stream of new development flowing out of the built-up urban areas and the substantial urban reconstruction, which hopefully may occur in the older urban centers.

Land Banking

Land banking is a form of advance land acquisition on a large scale. Widely used by the city of Stockholm in Sweden and adopted for use by several Canadian cities, public land banking can be found in the United States only in the Commonwealth of Puerto Rico. However, the tide seems to be moving strongly toward such a practice. Numerous commission and agency reports have recommended that a policy of land banking be adopted. In 1968, the National Commission on Urban Problems, for example, proposed

. . . that state governments enact legislation enabling state and/or local development authorities or agencies of general purpose government to acquire land in advance of development for the following purposes: (a) assuring the continuing availability of sites needed for development; (b) controlling the timing, location, type and scale of development; (c) preventing urban sprawl; and (d) reserving to the public gains in land values resulting from the action of government in promoting and servicing development.[11]

In addition to the advantages cited by the Douglas Commission, land banking can provide a method of reserving specific sites needed for public facilities. This tends to reduce capital costs and also to increase the opportunities of using public facility construction to guide development patterns. Perhaps most important, sites in the land bank can be released from time to time in accordance with development plans as well as market conditions. And, finally, land banking provides a simple and direct method of reserving open space to protect stream valleys, flood plains, and scenic areas.

Over a period of six decades (1904-1967), the city of Stockholm acquired approximately 134,000 acres of land on its outskirts for future development purposes. The practice proved so successful in the earlier years of the century that half of the land bank total was added in the decade of the 1960s.

Stockholm's experience with the use of this innovative instrument for the control of land use has significant implications for highly urbanized states such as New Jersey. By extending high-speed transit lines into outlying areas, Stockholm was able to generate development of a series of semiautonomous urban centers, each with its own shopping center, cultural facilities, and in some cases, industrial bases, grouped at high-density nodes around transit stations. These new urban centers are separated by tracts of wooded land rather than linked by endless rows of garish strip development, as is the New Jersey pattern. Stockholm's new town suburbs, noted for the high quality of their urban design, have become international models for urban planning.[12]

One recognized land-use expert recommends that an appropriate unit of government should, as a rule of thumb, acquire approximately 60 percent of the land in its general area for use 5, 10, or even 20 years ahead. He suggests that such land need not be kept idle but can be leased for interim periods.[13]

A number of cities in western Canada, including Calgary, Saskatoon, and Red Deer, have made extensive use of land banking techniques. Their successful experience with this technique led the Canadian Task Force on Housing and Urban Development in 1967 to recommend that land banking be adopted as general practice.

Municipalities or regional governments, as a matter of continuing policy, should acquire, service and sell all, or a substantial portion of the land required for urban growth within their boundaries.[14]

In 1962, the Puerto Rican legislature created the Puerto Rican Land Administration, and gave it broad powers to acquire land by purchase or condemnation. The Puerto Rican Land Administration was empowered to acquire land

. . . which may be kept in reserve towards facilitating the continuation of the development of public work and social and economic welfare programs which may be under way or which may be undertaken by the administration itself [or] by the Commonwealth of Puerto Rico . . . for the benefit . . . of the community, including, but not limited to, housing and industrial development programs.[15]

The primary impetus for this Puerto Rican legislation was the need to acquire sites for low- and moderate-income housing in a period of rapidly rising land prices. The legislation enabled the Land Administration to acquire substantial land holdings in 11 urban areas to be used for eventual planned development. The legislation has been tested in the Commonwealth courts with the Supreme Court of Puerto Rico rendering its decision in 1971. The basis of the decision was a lawsuit brought by the developer against the Land Administration, which had acquired two of his parcels in the San Juan area as a means of furthering the metropolitan plan. The developer sued, alleging that the land bank legislation was an unconstitutional use of public power. The trial court upheld the developer on the grounds that the legislation went beyond the present scope of public necessity. But, on appeal to the Supreme Court, the lower court was reversed. Concluding that the decision of the lower court was based on obsolete reasoning, the Supreme Court found that the decision

. . . responds to yesteryear which was characterized by the limited and restricted function of merely governmental acts. . . . It represents the stale individualistic concept of the exclusive right to the use, enjoyment and disposal of property by the owner, which no longer prevails, when it is necessary to confront it with the common good.[16]

On the mainland, the Puerto Rican approach to early land acquisition was adapted and expanded with the creation of the Urban Development Corporation (UDC) in New York. Among its other powers, the UDC can acquire land, if necessary, by condemnation within the framework of its general purpose to guide sound overall development. Although most of this state agency's land was acquired through purchase rather than eminent domain, in 1971 the UDC began to use its condemnation powers. In effect, Puerto Rico and the UDC have blazed a new trail in the concept of public acquisition of land for general development purposes far in advance of actual need.[17]

If the Puerto Rican precedent is upheld by Supreme Court decisions on the mainland, it would significantly broaden prevailing legal rulings that restrict the use of eminent domain power for advance land acquisition. For example, one issue concerns the imminence of advance land acquisition. Federal highway funds are available to finance takings for highway purposes as many as seven years in advance of actual construction. Only one state (Virginia), however, has established statutory maxima for advance highway takings—12 years for interstate highways and 10 years for other highways. In 1953, the Florida Supreme Court upheld the right of the city of Miami to take land for airport purposes and retain it without construction for over seven years. The court stated that "it is the duty of public officials to plan for the future" and it was probable that the plaintiff's land would be needed for airport expansion.[18] In a Hawaiian case, the court allowed the state to acquire land as part of a state office building complex, even though the state was unable to show how and when the land would be used for this purpose.[19]

From these and related cases, it can be concluded that there are almost no legislative guidelines as to maximum time periods for advance land acquisition, and that the courts have been generous in approving fairly long periods. The one exception to this conclusion is a Michigan case that involved a land taking by a local board of education (*Board of Education* v *Baczewski)*. The court held that there was no necessity for the taking, stating that the necessity requirement " . . . does not mean an indefinite, remote or speculative future necessity, but means a necessity now existing or to exist in the near future."[20] Although the Baczewski decision applied a "reasonable time" criterion to the power of condemnation, it left open the possibility of establishing a specific number of years, since planning of public facilities for the future varies with type of public need.

In addition to the time factor in advance land acquisition, there is also the issue of whether the condemning agency must have, at the time of taking, specific plans for use of the land. In an early decision (1923), the court appeared to require at least a minimum of planning on the part of the agency at the time of taking.[21] More recently, however, the courts have held that it is not necessary for a state to have plans and specifications prepared and funds available before it can take property for public use. The Florida airport case previously cited (1953) is one example. In another Florida case, the state Supreme Court upheld the right of the highway department to acquire a developer's property before he could build a planned housing project. The court held that there was adequate public necessity for the taking, even though at the time of condemnation, the state planned no public use of the land for at least two years, had no funds allocated for the road, had no fixed construction date or way of determining such a date, had no engineering plan, and had no drawing to show the manner in which the road would affect the property.[22]

Excess Condemnation: A Useful Extension of Eminent Domain

Excess condemnation is a special problem of eminent domain that relates to the condemnor's ability to take more land than is actually needed for a proposed public improvement. Although the land taken over and above that required is termed "excess," the additional taking is considered to be an inherent part of the improvement within the constitutional limitations of public purpose. Otherwise, excess condemnations would not be upheld by the courts.

There are three legal theories underlying the concept of excess condemnation, each of which can be illustrated by the example of a highway land taking. These are (1) protective or restrictive; (2) remnant; and (3) recoupment. In the case of the first theory, a highway agency may wish to take land adjoining the right-of-way to prevent uses that would interfere with the safety, utility, or beauty of the highway. Under the remnant theory, the highway agency may take an entire parcel, although only a portion of it may be required for actual highway construction to avoid leaving remnants of such size, shape, or condition as to be essentially useless for private purposes or to avoid the payment of severance damages. Finally, the highway agency may condemn property adjacent to the right-of-way for resale at a profit to reduce the overall cost of the highway project.[23]

The implications of using excess condemnation as a flexible

device under eminent domain are readily apparent in the case of land areas surrounding PUDs and new communities. As noted earlier, there is a basic inconsistency between the intensive planning required as a condition of approval for PUDs and new communities and the lack of similar planning for the fringe areas surrounding such major development. Through excess condemnation, it may be possible, for example, to protect the new highways leading into such areas from physical and visual blight and to provide buffer zones for the new developments. In addition, the recoupment feature of excess condemnation may enable the condemning authority to recapture some of the increase in land values that inevitably occurs in adjoining areas to offset infrastructure and service costs.[24]

Conservation of Scenic Easements

William H. Whyte is one of the leaders of the movement to alert the nation to the need for action to preserve open space. In a report published in 1962,[25] Whyte stated the basic rationale for conservation of scenic easements as an alternative to outright acquisition via taking or purchase. As Whyte summarized the dilemma, most of the remaining open space in metropolitan areas is in private ownership, and it would be economically infeasible to expect all of this extremely expensive land to be acquired for public purposes. As previously demonstrated, the zoning mechanism cannot assure that appropriate land will be retained as open space. Whyte suggested the use of the easement device as a middle ground for securing the continued retention of private property in open land uses to serve scenic or conservation objectives. The legal issues involved in the use of the easement device have been thoroughly explored in several law review articles published during the 1960s.[26]

There are two general types of conservation easements: positive and negative. The positive easement provides the public with the right to make some specified use of private property. In New York State, for example, 860 miles of fishing easements have been acquired along streams.

In the case of negative easement, the right of the owner to make certain uses of his land is purchased by the government. For example, owners of parcels in flood-prone areas may sell their right to construct buildings subject to flood damage. Wisconsin's purchase of "scenic easements" to preserve the scenic character of highways is an illustration of this approach. Since 1962, Wisconsin has been acquiring easements along major highways that prohibit the dumping of refuse, the erection of billboards, the destruction of streets and shrubs, the erection or alteration of buildings, and the commercial and industrial uses of land and buildings. Through 1964, the scenic easement program in Wisconsin averaged 43 dollars per acre with the actual purchase price amounting to slightly under 20 dollars and administrative costs comprising the remainder. The easements taken extended 350 feet on each side of the highway center line, unless some closer natural screen dictated smaller takings.

There are clear advantages for the use of the easement device in rural areas. As noted in Wisconsin, the cost tends to be relatively low and the land is kept on the tax rolls. In areas closer to the central city, the situation is quite different. On open sites in built-up urban areas, particularly if they are located close to a road, negative easements may be extremely expensive. For this reason, the easement device must be used at a very early stage, long before development pressures have begun to escalate the price of land. [27] Its use in most areas of New Jersey would therefore be limited.

In 1962, one author suggested that the utility of the acquisition of conservation easements and form of development rights as an instrument for controlling the future growth of urban areas is extremely limited.[28] More recent thinking, however, gives greater support to the possibility of using the development rights approach as a device for guiding urban growth.

4 Control of Land Development Through Taxation Policies

For more than a century, analysts of land-use development have repeatedly stressed the negative impact of property taxation practices in the United States. The bill of particulars levied against the property tax system was, and is, a long one. It has been charged among other things that property taxes do the following:

1. Discriminate against the poor, particularly renters.
2. Reward hit-and-run speculation at the expense of sound, orderly development.
3. Impede the regeneration of urban areas by placing a premium on underutilization of land.
4. Encourage the conversion of farm land to development in order to relieve the pressure on the farmer of fair market value taxation.
5. Generate intercommunity tax and service disparities as a consequence of wide community variations in per capita tax base.
6. Provide continuing sources of temptation in the exercise of discretionary assessing power.
7. Tend to give undue weight to fiscal zoning as a controlling element in guiding urban development patterns.[1]

The widespread recognition of the disadvantages of property taxes for land development has led to a persistent search for viable alternatives. Beginning with Henry George, the quest for a different and better form of land-use taxation dates back well over a century. However, no satisfactory replacement for the property tax system has yet been discovered, and the persisting dissatisfaction with this approach has led to the growing trend to edge away from property taxes as a major strategy for the financing of urban services. As pointed out by Dick Netzer, prior to the 1930s, three-fourths or more of the general revenue of local governments in the nation was derived from property taxes. By 1965-1966, this proportion had declined to just over 40 percent,[2] and partly as a consequence of liberalized state grants-in-aid and federal revenue sharing, property taxes as a proportion of local general revenue decreased even

43

further by 1973. Despite this downward trend, property taxation remains the bulwark of municipal finance and, as a consequence, continuing attention is still being given to alternatives for further reducing its significance in local taxation, on the one hand, and for using taxation powers as a positive tool for guiding urban development, on the other.

The fact that onerous tax burdens create serious land development problems in some respects has led to an overemphasis in some quarters on the relative significance of local tax rates in determining developmental trends. The decline of central cities, for example, has been partly ascribed to the fact that local property owners are heavily taxed as compared to those in the suburbs. In reality, however, recent experience has demonstrated that social factors (for example, high crime rates, poor schools) are the primary cause of central city decline, along with certain physical, environmental, and political detriments (for example, pollution, traffic congestion, deteriorating housing, dirty streets, and political corruption). Moreover, for certain kinds of property, including office buildings and luxury apartments, high property taxes are not a major component in the overall profit equation. Profit-oriented developers have constructed new offices and apartments in high tax communities throughout the nation. Perhaps a more accurate evaluation would be to note that high property taxes tend to aggravate other forces militating in the direction of decline. Persons and employers who have the option of leaving the central cities may wish to do so for a variety of reasons, and a high municipal tax bill may represent "the last straw." Conversely, communities attractive to relocators may have equally high tax rates but are also likely to enjoy offsetting advantages.

Constitutional Limitations.

Over the years a variety of adjustments have been recommended in the property tax system to mitigate its harmful effects and to provide incentives for developments deemed desirable. Invariably such proposals have encountered serious constitutional problems related mainly to the "equal and uniform" standards for taxation required by state constitutions.[3]

The "equal and uniform" constitutional requirements serve as a major barrier to both of the two principal types of property tax reform generally proposed. The first of these involves the classification of different categories of property, which are then taxed at different effective rates. For example, residential property might be taxed at a lower tax rate than commercial property. The second, site value taxation, shifts much, if not all, of the property tax away from improvements, for example, from building to land.

Property Tax Classification

Classification dates back at least two generations, but only two states have thus far adopted classification systems for the taxation of real property. Minnesota enacted its first classification statute in 1913 based on a constitutional amendment approved in 1907. Since the original enactment, which established four classes of property, the statute has been amended several times. In the late 1960s, the tax rate differential ranged from five percent of market value for rural electric lines to 50 percent for iron ore. Montana adopted a similar classification system in 1919. One of the special features of the Montana arrangement is the low rate of taxation extended to general unproductive property as compared with income-producing property.

Supporters of property tax classification contend that it provides a better measure of ability to pay, partly because it considers the income yield of property and also because it simplifies administration of the tax laws. Critics deny these claims for improvement and contend further that the abandonment of uniformity reduces total revenue and creates new injustices and inequities.

In New Jersey, the most recent study of tax policy recommended strongly against classification: "No program should be considered which would resort to classification of real estate or shrink the tax base further or distort its use to distribute the local burden. . . ."[4]

Site Value Taxation

More far-reaching than property tax classification is site value taxation, which is similar to Henry George's original proposal for a "single tax" on land and which has enjoyed something of a revival in recent years. There are three major arguments usually advanced in favor of this approach. The first, relating to equity, suggests that land values rise not because of the actions of individual land owners but because of external social, political, and economic forces, such as an increase in population, a rise in incomes, and an extension of public services. Under these circumstances, the public has a right to recoup increments in land values rather than permit them to be captured by the land owner. Secondly, it is claimed that taxing the unearned increment does no economic harm since it does not affect the supply of building sites nor does it remove any incentives to invest in new or renovated buildings. In contrast, traditional taxation practices penalize building construction and other improvements. Finally, say the proponents of site value taxation, relatively heavy taxes on land provide a significant inducement to spur building since development revenues are needed to offset the taxes on land. For this reason, it is suggested that heavy land taxes would discourage speculators from withholding land from the market. This assumption is supported by the fact that throughout the United States, taxes on buildings are disproportionately higher than taxes on land.

A professional economist extends the list of advantages for site value taxation to emphasize a series of related benefits derived from combining site value taxation with major aspects of the planning process. Mason Gaffney suggests the following ways in which land value taxation can reinforce good planning:

1. It gives planners a positive tool for influencing land use where they now have only negative powers.
2. It gives public investment great leverage over private investment, permitting public planners to take the initiative in development.
3. It gives planners some leverage over tax assessors.
4. It permits planners to plan for open space instead of allocating open space as a secondary by-product of land speculation. Tax pressures can be applied to assure early compact use of land between open spaces, to combat sprawl and crowding, and to safeguard open land.
5. It shortens the period between site renewal and provides an opportunity to synchronize demolitions and replanning.
6. It helps planners to emphasize neighborhood specialization and

differentiation, and gives greater assurance of equity in tax policy.

7. It leads to demand for greater variety in community facilities and fosters greater interdependence between the public and private sectors.[5]

Despite the manifold claims for the great advantages of site value taxation, some observers cite significant defects in its actual practice. One critic contends that site value taxation does not conform nearly as well as composite taxation to three important principles of taxation—(1) the ability to pay; (2) benefits received, and (3) stability. Ability to pay falters, for example, when an empty parcel of land is taxed as heavily as an adjoining site containing a large, revenue-yielding structure. The "benefits received" principle can be viewed in two ways. The owner of a large building that generates considerable vehicular and pedestrian traffic should be taxed more heavily than the owner of an empty parcel with little or no impact on municipal services. Moreover, some public services provided to property owners (sewers, sidewalks, driveways) are actually financed through special assessments or betterments and consequent increases in land values are not the result of unearned increment. As for the principle of taxation stability, land fluctuates substantially in value from year to year, and a tax system based on a composite of land and buildings provides a more secure foundation for municipal tax policy. The most telling blow to site value taxation came during The Great Depression when a number of municipalities in western Canada were forced to retreat from this practice because shrinking revenues from declining land values provided insufficient funds to support debt service.[6]

In New Jersey, the State Tax Policy Committee recently gave cautious approval for site value taxation and recommended an experimental program on a meaningful option basis for cities of over 100,000 population. This conclusion and recommendation were based on Netzer's findings in New York City and several New Jersey municipalities. The Tax Policy Committee gave guarded approval for the adoption of site value taxation only by the state's sorely troubled larger cities for the purpose of encouraging new private investment. The Committee felt, however, that site value taxation was not applicable as tax policy for other areas of the state, including PUDs, new communities, and their environs. In particular, the Tax Policy Committee emphasized that site value taxation, by shifting tax values to land, would run counter to other policies, such as the Farmland Assessment Act, which seeks to preserve open space through preferential tax assessment.[7]

Graded Property Tax Plan: Scranton and Pittsburgh Approach

The graded property tax is a modified version of the classification and site value taxation schemes previously discussed. In 1913, during the heyday of the Henry George "single tax" movement, the cities of Pittsburgh and Scranton in Pennsylvania were authorized to shift to a so-called graded property tax over a 12-year period. (It should be pointed out that the Pennsylvania constitution contains relatively liberal provisions on "equal and uniform" taxation standards.) Since 1925, land in these two cities has been taxed at twice the rate of improvements. But because this arrangement applies only to city property taxes, not to county or school district tax levies, the actual rate of taxation for improvements in Pittsburgh was 71 percent of the rate for land in 1960. Although legislation enacted in 1951 and 1959 extended the graded property tax option to 48 other municipalities (excluding Philadelphia), few have taken advantage of this opportunity. Arguments advanced for and against the graded property tax plan are similar to those revolving around the general single tax system.

Constitutionally Acceptable Modifications in Property Taxes

Over the years, the courts have approved exceptions from the "equal and uniform" taxation standards under the rubric of achieving special vital public purposes. For example, state legislatures have granted special property tax advantages to identifiable groups, including farmers, veterans, the aged, to eleemosynary institutions, and to low- and moderate-income families in need of housing.

Preferential Farmland Assessment

Farmers, particularly those with acreage on the urban fringe, are particularly vulnerable to rising property taxes. Their taxes increase far beyond their income as development pressures intensify, land is reassessed, and property tax rates rise. Caught in this financial squeeze, they find it hard to resist offers made by developers, which promise relief from high taxes and substantial cash profits. On the assumption that farmland provides valuable open space, particularly around the urban fringe, 19 states have adopted preferential assessment statutes, which authorize the assessment of agricultural land at use value rather than fair market value.

In New Jersey, the Farmland Assessment Act of 1964 provides for the preferential assessment of "land . . . actively devoted to agricultural or horticultural use" at its value for use rather than at its value on the real estate market. There are certain conditions governing this granting of preferential assessment: (1) The site must be not less than five acres; (2) it must be in single ownership; and (3) gross annual sales of farm products must achieve a modest, that is, $500 level. In addition, when the use changes to nonfarm use, there is a rollback tax due from the seller equal to the difference actually paid and the amount that would have been paid under normal assessing procedures for the year of change and the two preceeding years.

The New Jersey Tax Policy Committee concluded that the state's farmland preferential assessment act has had little impact in decelerating the conversion of farmland for urban development. In 1971 preferential assessments under the act amounted to only $7.4 million. Between 1964 and 1969, farm acreage in the state declined by 10 percent and a 1967 survey by Rutgers University found that a majority of farmers surveyed indicated that the act had no influence on their decisions on whether to sell their land. In addition, the Committee heard complaints concerning corporations that purchase large farm holdings near urban areas and qualify for preferential assessment by producing minimal amounts of crops.[8]

Housing Tax Abatements

Most state legislatures have enacted a series of special property tax concessions for the purposes of stabilizing and subsidizing housing costs for low- and moderate-income families. For example, in New Jersey, local housing authorities pay 10 percent of their rent rolls in lieu of taxes to the municipalities where they are sited. In addition, housing development for middle-income families are entitled to special tax arrangements under three statutes:

1. Limited dividend housing corporations may pay 15 percent of rent to municipalities in lieu of taxes.
2. Urban renewal corporations may pay 15 percent of rents in lieu of taxes for shorter periods of time under the Fox-Lance formula.
3. Projects, the mortgages of which are insured by the New Jersey Housing Finance Agency (HFA), either under its own statutory provisions or under the Fox-Lance formula, are eligible for payments in lieu of taxes of 20 percent or less. Most HFA developments in practice receive tax abatements at the 15-percent-of-rent level.

Senior citizens are widely considered a specially deserving hardship group whose low retirement income does not permit them to absorb local tax increases. Under special provisions of the state constitution and law, resident property owners over 65 years of age with annual incomes under $5000 are granted $160 reductions per year in their property tax bills. Half the cost of this program is borne by the municipalities, half by the state.

The state constitution grants qualified New Jersey war veterans a $50 per year reduction from their property tax bills. In 1971, these property tax abatements amounted to $22.3 million, or 1.7 percent of the gross tax levied on real estate.

In reviewing the several categories of property tax abatements and exemptions, the New Jersey Tax Policy Commission concluded that the state was penalizing municipalities at little cost to the state and that, in consequence, major revisions and, in the case of veterans' exemptions, outright repeal was in order. In effect, these abatements amounted to an erosion of the local tax base and a shifting of the tax burden in an inequitable and indefensible manner.[9]

Alternate Approaches in Use of Taxing Power

The initial portions of this chapter discussed the general impact of the property tax system on land development and concluded with an analysis of the direct use of the tax system to achieve land-use and housing objectives. This portion of the chapter is devoted to an examination of the deliberate use of the taxing power in other states as a means of achieving land-use objectives. As will be subsequently noted, there is a direct parallel between New Jersey's effort to protect its farmland through preferential tax incentives and the broad tax programs adopted in a few states to assist in guiding overall land-use development. As one authority suggests, tax policies are too often in direct conflict with land-use objectives, but corrective mechanisms can be adopted to convert tax policy into an incentive rather than a deterrent.[10]

Hawaiian Approach

One of the rare examples of a "marriage of the land taxes and the planners" exists in the state of Hawaii.[11] Under Hawaiian legislation, mostly adopted in 1961 and 1963, a statewide Land Use Commission is authorized to classify all land in the state into one of four major districts: urban, rural, agricultural, and conservation. The urban districts include a reasonable area of expansion; the counties administer planning and zoning for all but the conservation districts, which are under state control; the state commission determines uses in the agricultural districts although counties may allow other uses by special permit. Tax maps showing the land-use districts based on county planning and zoning determinations are furnished to tax assessors. Since the assessors give consideration in establishing value to potential use as well as current use, this has the effect of implementing general land-use plans. For example, areas zoned for extensive uses tend to be lightly taxed while areas designated for intensive development are taxed more heavily.[12]

In addition to this novel land-use taxation approach, the Hawaii tax statutes also provide that land used for "specific ranching or other agricultural use" may be "dedicated" to that use, and receive preferential agricultural assessment for taxation purposes, even if the land is located in an urban district. To be so "dedicated," such land must have been used "in an intensive agricultural use" for five years preceding the dedication and the owner forfeits the right to change the land use for at least 10 years. From 1963 to 1969, 760 petitions for dedication were processed, resulting in grants for preferential assessment amounting to almost 18,000 acres, roughly 1 percent of the state's total land area. The granting of preferential assessment meant a 48 percent decrease in valuation for the dedicated land. When dedicated land is finally developed, the owner is responsible for all back taxes that would have been paid at fully assessed valuation plus 5 percent interest.[13]

California Land Conservation Act

As noted earlier, 19 states have adopted preferential taxation measures aimed mainly at keeping farmland in agricultural use. In some of these states, the protected farming operations were of marginal utility and their elimination from agricultural production would not have had much impact. Farming in California is a different proposition. That state's 7 million acres of prime farmland produce 42 percent of the nation's fruits and nuts, 43 percent of its vegetables, and almost 100 percent of many of its specialty crops.

Prior to adoption of California's Land Conservation Act of 1965, farmland was being withdrawn from agricultural use at the rate of 150,000 acres per year. Earlier efforts to establish a preferential taxation system for farmland in 1957 and 1962 were declared unconstitutional because of constitutional requirements that "land be assessed at its true value in money." Legislation of 1965 and 1966 moved in a different direction, linking the granting of preferential taxation to the land-use planning process. These later measures established the principles (1) that preferential assessments could be granted for open space land as defined by the legislature, and (2) that such preferences would only be extended to land subject to enforceable restrictions. As noted, the concept of open land was expanded far beyond farmland to include many other types of open space: managed wetland areas, scenic highway corridors, wildlife habitat areas, ponds, and submerged areas.

The Land Conservation Act and its 1966 and 1969 amendments were based on Constitutional Article XXVII adopted by the voters in 1966. In addition, new sections (421-425) of the State Revenue and Taxation Code were formulated to implement the taxation features of the open space legislation. Under the revised California legislation, areas of land may be classified as "agricultural preserves" by counties if the areas are at least 100 acres in size and are shown in the county general plan. Within such agricultural preserves, land uses are to be limited to agricultural or "compatible" uses as determined by the county. Once agricultural preserves are established, counties may enter into enforceable restrictions with land owners that bind the land to existing agricultural or open space uses for a term of 10 years. The contract is renewed automatically each year unless notice is served to terminate, in which case the contract expires nine years from the date of notification. In return, the owner receives a tax assessment based on the restricted use of the land under the contract; when he sells such land, he is penalized not by a tax rollback, as under the New Jersey Farmland Assessment Act, but by a penalty equal to 50 percent of the full cash value of the land in its unrestricted use. California's Land Conservation Act also provides for scenic restrictions and open space easements. Moreover, it includes a series of restrictions and prohibitions on takings of open space land by public agencies.

As of May 1970, almost 5.9 million acres of land in California (six out of every 100 acres in the state) had been placed under enforceable restrictions. Most of this land was in outlying areas—only 6.4 percent was located within three miles of urban centers. Thus, most of the land-use contracts have been established in outlying areas less subject to intense development pressures. For this reason, supplementary measures may be needed in addition to this tax incentive to provide open space in the areas contiguous to the urban fringe.[14]

Vermont

Although the state of Vermont has been noted for its dairy production—for many years it had more cows than people—most of its farmland was considered only marginally profitable and much of it has been abandoned over the last century. Thus, Vermont, unlike California, lacked the urgent agricultural rationale for preserving open space. Instead, Vermonters have been primarily concerned with the ecological (and social) impact of a sizable influx of out-of-state vacationers, purchasers of second homes, and land developers, whose activities were bidding up the prices of land and causing substantial environmental damage.[15]

Vermont has attempted to confront this problem by enacting a series of environmental impact and related taxation measures. In terms of environmental control, developers must now demonstrate that their proposals will meet a long list of environmental criteria. As for taxation, a new Vermont approach combines capital gains taxation on land, designed to combat short-term land speculation, with tax relief for property owners based on progressive gradations of income. Effective May 1, 1973, Vermont applied a capital gains tax ranging from 5 to 60 percent on land sales. Applicable to all land sales, except those of one acre or less that are used as a principal residence, the capital gains tax rate is computed for the period of time the land is held prior to sale and the amount of profit measured as a percentage of tax cost. A companion taxation measure gives property tax relief through credits for property taxes paid in excess of a graduated percentage of household income. "Both measures are designed to exercise some control over speculation in the use and market value of land in Vermont."[16] Yields from the two tax measures are linked together in that revenue from the capital gains legislation is being used to finance part of the cost of providing property tax relief.

Conclusions

Experience with preferential taxation policies to protect and conserve open space in the states that have adopted such legislation suggests that this is only a first step in making maximum utilization of taxation as an instrument for guiding development. One basic conclusion is that taxation policies must be grounded on and closely linked to a regional or state land-use plan. Of the states that adopted preferential taxation, only Hawaii specifically attempted to integrate taxation with planning. As noted in this report, however, Hawaii not only failed to update its land-use plans but, in practice, its tax officials frequently overlook the prevailing land-use classifications.

California is the most responsive and effective state model, partly because the state has used its experience to revise its legislation continually to eliminate weak and ineffectual statutory provisions. A 1970 report suggested further expansion of the legislation to include "open space," which would be identified and protected in the public interest, in addition to the farmland currently protected. The report also recommended that special "development planning contracts" be used as a means of implementing long-range land-use plans in land adjacent to built-up urban areas. It is in these close-in areas that development pressures are the greatest and that efforts to preserve open land have proved least effective.[17]

5

Preservation of Open Space Through the Transfer of Development Rights

Precedent for Transferability of Development Rights

The transfer of development rights as a means of controlling the use and development of land is not without precedent. Almost three decades of British experimentation in land-use control has been based upon this concept. In the United States, there are numerous illustrations of judicial recognition of its existence and sanction of its validity. Examination of these precedents is useful to an understanding of the concept.

The British Experiment[1]

In the late 1930s and early 1940s, the British Parliament, concerned with the need to decentralize and disperse industries and industrial population, to redevelop congested urban areas, and to decrease the vulnerability of population and industry to air attack, created three committees to study and report on these problems and their solution. Extensive studies by these committees resulted in three now famous reports: (2) the *Barlow Report*[2]; (2) the *Uthwatt Report*[3]; and (3) the *Scott Report*[4]. Considered together, these reports proposed that land-use planning be on a national scale, that private rights in land be subjected to the public welfare, and that the use of land by private owners be restricted to accomplish this objective.[5]

Of the three reports, the *Uthwatt Report* made the most significant contributions to the field of land-use regulation in its conceptualization of the problem and its recommendations for solutions. The *Uthwatt Report* defined and emphasized the importance of several new land-use concepts including (1) *betterment* and (2) *floating value*.

Betterment was defined as an increase in the value of land that results when government undertakes public works or other improvements on adjacent or nearby land. This concept included "the principle that persons whose property has clearly been increased in market value by an improvement effected by local authorities should specially contribute to the cost of the improvement."[6] *Betterment charge* is the term describing the exaction by which government recoups this increment in market value.

Floating value was defined as the potential increase in value of all undeveloped land in an area. In the early stages of development of an area, predicting with any certainty the exact parcels of land upon which the floating value will settle is practically impossible. Public control of land use, however, results in the shifting of floating value from some sections of land to other sections.

After analyzing the nature and implications of these concepts, the Uthwatt committee recommended, *inter alia,* that:

1. A system be established to "recoup the betterment" from land-owners who are "unjustly enriched" by increases in value of their land resulting from government action and to compensate landowners from whose land the "floating value" had been shifted by governmental action.

2. The rights of development in all land lying outside built-up areas (with certain exceptions) be vested immediately in the government and that fair compensation be paid for those rights. Thereafter, such land could not be developed without the consent of the government and the repurchase of the development right.

The Uthwatt committee believed that these (and other) recommendations would achieve the benefits of government control of land use without government nationalization (ownership) of the land. The device that was proposed to accomplish this objective was the separation of the development right from the other rights of ownership of land and the transfer of that right to government.

Parliament adopted these recommendations in the Town and County Planning Act of 1947[7] (hereinafter called the 1947 Act). Under this law, the British government took over the development rights of all undeveloped land. This left the owners of land with all other rights of ownership, except the right to develop.[8] When an owner wanted to develop his land, he had to buy back the right to develop from the government by paying a development charge.

The 1947 Act provides for compensation to landowners for the value of the development right at the time of the taking in 1947. The amount of the compensation was set at the value of the land in excess of "existing uses" as defined in the statute. A 300 million pound revolving fund was created from which compensation would be paid and into which the betterment charges would be deposited.

In spite of the hopes and best intentions of planners and legislators, it is generally conceded that the system did not work well in practice,[9] primarily because owners "refused to develop their land or sell it for anything less than its full market value."[10] Buyers who would have to pay a development charge in an amount equal to the difference between the current market value and the 1947 "existing use" value would be willing to pay for land no more than the 1947 "existing use" value. It soon became apparent that the price that sellers demanded and the price that developers could pay for land was so far apart that the marketability of land had been destroyed. Consequently, Parliament abolished the development charge in the Town and Country Planning Acts of 1953 and 1954.[11] This legislation did not return the development rights to the land owners. The law only eliminated the charge previously exacted for permission to develop. The development rights remained separated from the rest of the rights of land ownership.

Then, in 1967, in an extremely intricate and complex [12] piece of legislation,[13] the development charge was reinstated at 40 percent of the "development value" (not unlike our capital gains tax) and remained in effect until 1971 when it was abolished once again.[14]

The British experience with development rights has been something less than a resounding success. The development rights are still separated from the balance of the title and have been retained by the British government. Thus far, the British have been unable to devise an effective system by which the separation and marketability of development rights may be used as a land-use control device.

American Experience

The American experience with development rights transfer is less specific, more diverse, less systematized, and more recent than the British. Nevertheless, the development rights transfer concept has been used in the United States in such programs as: (1) eminent domain acquisition of less than a full fee; (2) landmark preservation transfer of floor-area ratio (FAR) rights; and (3) incentive zoning transfer of FAR bonuses.

Eminent Domain Acquisition of Less Than the Fee. There are both judicial and legislative precedents for government acquisition of less than the fee simple.[15] One of the original proponents of government acquisition of less than the fee simple used the phrase "conservation easement" to describe the part of the title acquired by government.[16] The use of the word "easement" to describe this legal right was an unfortunate choice of nomenclature because of numerous technical common law restrictions on easements. Two such common law principles are: (1) the law will not recognize the creation of new kinds of easements[17]; (2) the benefits of easements are generally not assignable[18], and, where assignable, may not be separated from the land benefited therefrom.[19] In spite of these common law rules, American courts have recognized the right of government agencies to acquire less than the full fee under varied circumstances. For example, the Minnesota Supreme Court upheld the "taking" of the right to build certain classes of buildings in areas where such restriction was necessary to assure fit and harmonious surrounding for residential use.[20] In California, a court upheld the condemnation of the right of joint use of utility line poles. The court conceded that there was no precise legal designation for the right being acquired, but it said that wherever a substantial right of use exists, that right is subject to the power of eminent domain.[21] In New York, a court upheld the condemnation of interests in strips of land next to a highway that left the owner of the fee with little more than the right to use the land for ornamental courtyards only. The court held that the city should limit its taking to only that legal interest required to meet the public need.[22]

The legislatures of several states, as previously indicated, have begun to recognize the advantage of acquiring interests in land for less than the full fee. The New Jersey Green Acres Land Acquisition Act of 1961 provided that:

Without limitation of the definition of "lands" herein, the commissioner may acquire, or approve grants to assist a local unit to acquire . . . an interest or right consisting, in whole or in part, of a *restriction* on the use of land by others including owners of other interests therein. . . .[23]

The New Jersey statute describes the right to be taken in negative terms, that is, authorization is granted to acquire a "restriction on the use of land." This self-conscious discomfort with the concept also appears, but to a lesser extent, in the wording of the California statute:

Any county or city may acquire, by purchase, gift, grant devise, lease, or otherwise, and through the expenditure of public funds, the fee, *or any lesser interest or right* in real property in order to preserve, *through* limitation of their future use, open spaces and areas for public use and enjoyment.[24]

On the other hand, authors of the Vermont statute seem to have overcome any insecurity with this new concept and have expressly recognized development rights in their eminent domain enabling legislation:

The legislative body of a municipality or a department, as the case may be, shall determine the types of rights and interest, equitable servitudes, profits, rights under covenants, easements, *development rights,* or any other rights and interests in real property of whatever character.[25]

As American planners and attorneys became familiar with the concept of the transferability of development rights, they began to experiment with techniques by which the concept might be used as a land-use control device. This effort has moved in two directions to date: (1) preservation of landmarks, and (2) incentive (bonus) zoning.

Transfers of FAR Rights to Preserve Historic Landmarks. One student of urban affairs has compared urban landmarks to the ocelot and the snow leopard because all are "imperiled species."[26] Attempts to preserve urban landmarks by police power prohibition of their demolition have been held to violate the constitutional protection against unreasonable deprivation of property.[27] On the other hand, municipal resources are chronically insufficient to fund the acquisition of urban landmarks through the eminent domain power. This dilemma has provided the incentive for some cities, including New York City and Chicago, to experiment with the transfer of development rights as a means of preserving urban landmarks.[28]

The New York City ordinance provides:

The City Planning Commission may permit *development rights* to be transferred to adjacent lots from lots occupied by landmark buildings . . . and may permit in the case of residential developments or enlargements, the minimum required open space or the minimum lot area per room to be reduced on the basis of such transfer of development rights.[29]

The New York City transfer of development rights system is based upon the fact that the value of real estate in many parts of the city depends upon the intensity of development permitted under the zoning law and the fact that urban landmarks usually have an excess of authorized but unbuilt floor-area ratio (FAR) provisions. The FAR is a zoning technique to regulate the physical volume (density) of a building by controlling the relation between the floor area of a building and the area of the lot on which the building stands.[30]
Expressed as a formula:

$$\text{PAR (5)} = \frac{\text{Floor Area} \quad (50{,}000 \text{ square feet})}{\text{Lot Area} \quad (10{,}000 \text{ square feet})}$$

Thus, a building to be constructed in a zoning district with an FAR of 5 could have five times more floor space than lot area. Consequently, an owner of a lot of 10,000 square feet could build no more than 50,000 square feet of floor space. If that parcel is in an area with sufficient economic demand for more intensive development, for example, high-rise office construction, the owner would seek to find ways to increase the floor area of his proposed building. The New York City ordinance permits landmark owners to sell the authorized but unused floor area of their landmark site to adjacent lot owners. Consequently, the owner of an adjacent lot may purchase the unused floor area from the landmark owner. The consideration for this transfer of "development rights" compensates the landmark owner for preserving the landmark. Once the landmark owner transfers the development rights (that is, authorized but unused floor area), the incentive to demolish the landmark is reduced because of the limited floor area authorization still remaining for use on the landmark site.
The New York City system of development right transfer has not been widely used or successful in preserving the city's landmarks. [31] The Chicago ordinance seeks to improve upon this system by a more ambitious and comprehensive program. Under the Chicago plan, (1) transfers of development rights are not limited to adjacent properties. Transfers are permitted to any property within specially

created development rights transfer districts; (2) an attempt is made to compensate the landmark owner for the actual cost of preserving the landmark structure, including the right to transfer up to 100 percent of the FAR, as well as real estate tax reduction and special municipal subsidies, where necessary. Nevertheless, the primary incentive is the transfer of development rights from one land to another. The Chicago plan stops short of a general bonus system for favored improvements.

Incentive (Bonus) Zoning. The logical extension of the New York City and Chicago programs, where development rights are transferred from one owner to another, is a general bonus system where a bonus FAR is created by the municipality. The City of San Francisco has adopted such a system.[32] Under this plan, the downtown is divided into four districts, each with a prescribed FAR. A builder may obtain a bonus of an increased FAR, within prescribed limits, by providing public benefits such as: (1) improved accessibility (for example, rapid transit access, rapid transit proximity, parking access); (2) improved pedestrian movement (for example, multiple building entrances, sidewalk widening, shortened walking distances); (3) pedestrian amenities (for example, a plaza); (4) light and air for streets (for example, additional setbacks or low coverage on upper floors); (5) view enhancement (for example, an observation deck).[33]

In a strict sense, the San Francisco plan and other programs of incentive zoning that offer FAR bonuses are not examples of the transfer of development rights because a part of the fee is not separated from the title of one landowner and transferred to another landowner. Instead, the government, under its police power, artificially restricts development and then prescribes conditions under which those restrictions may be relaxed. On the other hand, the San Francisco plan is similar to the rights of development system in that the right to develop is specifically singled out, among the other rights of ownership, and manipulated as a device to control land use. For this reason, awareness of the incentive bonus system, as well as the landmark preservation system and the British experiments, is helpful in understanding the newer proposals to use the transfer and marketability of development rights as a means of preserving open space.

Proposed Legislation to Utilize Development Rights
Marketability and Transfers to Preserve Open Space

The first legislative attempt to create a comprehensive system in
which the marketability and transfer of development rights are used
to regulate land use was introduced in the Maryland Senate in 1972
by State Senator William Goodman.[34] At the same time, in New
Jersey, a committee made up of Rutgers University faculty and
members of the New Jersey Department of Community Affairs were
independently engaged in a similar project.[a] The provisions set forth
below are excerpts, with modifications of the legislative proposal
that emerged, from that committee.[35] This draft does not purport to
be a complete or final draft of a legislative proposal. It is designed
primarily as a device to draw attention to the possibilities for the use
of the concept and to the problems that require solution.

Summary of the Legislative Proposal

The proposed legislation seeks to utilize the separability and transferability of development rights as the basis of a technique to induce
owners of undeveloped land to preserve their land in open space.
The owners of preserved open space are compensated for their
deprivation of use by the sale of development rights to developers of
other land in the jurisdiction. To make such sales possible, it is
necessary to establish a system that creates a market for development rights in which owners of developable land must buy development rights from owners of preserved open space land as a prerequisite for development.

The legislation is designed to create such a market in the following manner:

1. Each local government would prepare a land-use plan that
specifies the percentage of remaining undeveloped land in the jurisdiction and that designates the land to remain undeveloped as preserved open space land. The land-use plan would also designate the
land to be developed and would specify the uses to which the
developable land may be put. A zoning law would be enacted or
amended to implement this plan.

---

[a]Members of this committee were T. Airola, R. Binetsky, B. Chavooshian, R. Ginman, T.
Hall, J. Jager, T. Norman, E. Reoch, and J. Rose.

2. The planning board of each local government would prescribe the number of development rights required for each housing unit to be developed. On the basis of this numerical assignment, the planning board wold then compute the number of development rights required to develop the jurisdiction in accordance with the land-use plan. The local government would issue certificates of development rights (ownership of which would be recorded) in the exact amount so determined.

3. Every owner of preserved open space land would receive certificates of development rights in an amount that represents the percentage of assessed value of his undeveloped land to the total assessed value of all undeveloped land in the jurisdiction.

4. An owner of developable land, who desires to develop his land more intensively (for example, apartments instead of single family residence) would have to buy additional development rights, on the open market, from those who have acquired such rights from either original distribution or subsequent purchase.

5. Thus, owners of preserved open space would be able to sell their development rights to owners of developable land (or real estate brokers or speculators). In return for the compensation derived from this sale, owners of preserved open space land will have sold their rights to develop their land in the future. Their land will thus be preserved in open space and the owners will have been compensated without any capital costs to government.

6. Development rights will be subject to *ad valorem* property taxation as a component of the total assessed value of the developable real property in the jurisdiction.

For a detailed description and commentary on proposed development rights legislation for New Jersey, see the Appendix to this report.[36]

6

Allocation of Government Responsibility For Control of Land Development

Planned unit developments and new communities, like the smallest of subdivisions, come within the jurisdictional sphere of the municipality where they are located. It is primarily local government officials who engage in the intricate negotiating process that culminates in the ultimate development agreement. Other levels of government, however, particularly the state government, play major roles in guiding, shaping, and controlling local land-use decisions. The significance of these actions by higher levels of government for local land-use planning, for example, the location and timing of the construction of major highways, is often not readily apparent. However, local communities, developers, and prospective home purchasers are well aware of the relative importance of the presence or absence of good highway access in governing their decisions. In recent years, the influence of state government has been more strongly and directly felt, partly as a consequence of growing understanding of the secondary and tertiary consequences of the development programs of functional state agencies and prospective large-scale developers. In addition, there is an increasing tendency to shift land-use responsibilities from lower to higher levels of government to prevent and repair what are perceived as the undesirable consequences of parochially oriented municipal land-use planning or nonplanning. Finally, the state government, prodded by the courts and the federal government, has been rapidly moving in the direction of intervening in local land-use patterns for the purpose of providing higher levels of environmental quality and special assistance in meeting the needs of the disadvantaged for housing, schools, and neighborhood services. Both the state and federal governments have extended various financial incentives to municipalities, as well as to sponsors and developers, in return for meeting the criteria specified in land-use, environmental, and housing programs.

The previous chapters focused on the substantive aspects of existing alternative tools for guiding land-use development. This chapter concentrates on jurisdictional problems and issues involved in sorting out appropriate governmental levels for formulating and implementing land-use policy. It will become apparent in the discussion that follows that the allocation of land-use responsibilities among and within governmental jurisdictions is one of the most sensitive and controversial questions confronting the American governmental system, not only because these issues involve difficult trade-offs between development and environmental protection, but because the allocation of land-use powers impinges directly on such basic value-laden matters as home rule, the mixing of race and class, neighborhood versus integrated schools, and the possible intrusion of high-risk population groups into homogeneous stable communities.

Existing Allocation of Governmental Responsibilities

Role of Local Government

As noted previously in this report, New Jersey (and all states except Hawaii) has delegated virtually all governmental responsibility over land use to its 567 local governments. As elsewhere in the nation, this fragmentation of responsibility has resulted in a patchwork pattern of urban development exacerbated by relentless competition for ratables to ease the tax burden on homeowners. The complexity of the development pattern is aggravated by New Jersey's special demographic nature. Unlike the pattern in many other states, there is no single large metropolitan area in New Jersey containing half or more of the state's population. In states with a dominant metropolis, there tends to be a fairly regular arrangement of core cities surrounded by suburbs, which in turn gives way to exurban and outlying communities. New Jersey, with its diffuse system of urbanization, contains a number of small and medium-sized core cities located in fairly close proximity, with each municipality containing its own suburban and exurban zones, and the whole forming an intricate and overlapping configuration. Under these circumstances, effective coalitions of core-city political leaders, to serve as spokesmen for the most seriously problem-ridden municipalities become extremely necessary and extremely difficult to form, as well. This kind of fragmentation encourages tendencies toward apathy, inertia, and deep resistance to jurisdictional change.

One of the consequences of political fragmentation in a state that makes municipal planning and zoning permissive rather than mandatory is that many communities seek to avoid the trouble and expense of developing land-use control capability. This is particularly true of small, outlying semirural communities. As of 1973, a substantial number of municipalities had failed to enact planning ordinances, and over 100 had not yet adopted master plans. Many local governments did not even have zoning ordinances. While these statistics provide a quantitative yardstick of land-use control activity at the local level, they do not offer adequate criteria for gauging the quality and performance of communities that display only the requisite outward signs of planning and zoning operations. These weaknesses are particularly relevant to this study because PUDs and new communities, for obvious reasons, tend to locate on larger tracts of open lands in communities that heretofore have escaped the need for extensive and sophisticated planning inputs.

Municipal land-use controls have been attacked both in central cities and suburban communities on the grounds of undue parochialism and undesirable consequences. In the built-up core cities, the principal weakness lies in the ineffectiveness of the planning and zoning process: through exceptions granted by local appellate bodies, planning and zoning principles are constantly eroded for the benefit of individual property owners. The long-term cumulative result is often the negation of substantial elements of the officially accepted zoning map and land-use plan. In the suburbs, on the other hand, the planning-zoning process has the contrary attribute of working all too well in protecting and preserving the community as a whole against the intrusion of immigrants regarded as undesirables. While the consequences would not be so harmful if the practices were limited to a few communities, the fact is that exclusionary tactics have been widely adopted. The consequences of local control over zoning and planning have been successfully summarized by the former president of the New Jersey Bar Association, who also places much of the blame on the state's overreliance on real estate taxation.

1. It has produced zoning patterns which effectively exclude the disadvantaged from the suburbs by imposing restrictive lot sizes and square foot housing requirements, and by excluding publicly assisted housing.

2. It has produced zoning patterns which have attracted commercial and industrial ratables from the older cities to low population, low density suburbs.

3. It has isolated the new suburbs from the necessity for contributing to services needed by the poor, and left older cities to cope with their only revenue resource—a contracting real estate valuation base.

4. It has left the disadvantaged blue collar worker isolated in older cities remote from the growing areas of the state's industrial economy which might have provided blue collar job opportunities.

5. As older cities lost industrial and commercial ratables they provided reduced municipal services and declining job opportunities. At the same time, the rural poor, largely black, displaced by agricultural technology, provided a steady market for the obsolete housing plant remaining in the cities.[1]

As pointed out previously in this study, the almost complete delegation of land-use control powers to local government not only leads to the neglect of regional and state goals and impacts, but also often has unpleasant consequences for neighboring communities. The tendency to locate necessary but unsightly municipal installations, such as dumps, incinerators, and cemeteries as close as possible to an unfortunate neighbor, is one frequent product of this kind of behavior. A reverse consequence is the tendency of communities to shun and ban the location of much needed but undesired state and regional installations within their boundaries, for example, state homes for the mentally retarded, regional incinerators, community-based drug and alcoholism treatment centers, and regional airports. The stronger, politically influential communities tend to deflect such installations in the direction of their weaker neighbors.

Role of County Government

Ordinarily, weaknesses and problems attributable to governmental fragmentation and parochialism are moved up to the next higher level of government. In New Jersey this jurisdiction would be the county. However, county government in New Jersey is too feeble to serve as an effective arbiter or control agent for achieving regional land-use and land-development objectives. The legal, fiscal, political, and administrative inadequacies of county government have been fully explored by the Musto Commission, whose findings have been alluded to earlier in this report.[2] In the area of land use, the county and regional planning agencies have limited powers. They conduct research, serve in advisory capacities to the county freeholders and municipal agencies, and increasingly offer technical planning assistance to understaffed local governments. They also provide largely *pro forma* review of grant proposals on behalf of federal agencies. As federal revenue sharing expands, however, this review function is likely to diminish in importance.

The extent to which county government in New Jersey is perceived as essentially politically powerless, with little potential for evolving into an effective instrument for controlling land use, is displayed in the 1969 legislative proposal for a comprehensive planning and zoning enabling act. While this bill showed enormous deference to the principle and practice of home rule, it gave no additional land-use powers to county government. Furthermore, the proposed 1972 community planning act, a "watered down" version of the 1969 bill, similarly failed to strengthen the land-use control responsibilities of county and regional planning agencies.[3] Indicative of this attitude toward county government is the provision calling for the county planning board "to encourage cooperation" of municipalities on matters concerning the county master plan.[4] These planning and zoning legislative proposals fail to give counties the right to veto or even delay municipal land-use decisions other than those relating to county roads and sewerage facilities, powers that the counties already have.

Role of State Government

Land-use development problems arise in part from local fragmentation and parochialism, problems with which county and regional mechanisms have proved unable to cope. This has led to increasing demands for state intervention.[5] State government has been called upon to arbitrate intermunicipal land-use disputes; to provide technical assistance to local planning agencies; to protect selected ecologically vulnerable areas such as open spaces, flood plains, coastal zones and wetlands; and to take the leadership in evolving land-use policies based on broad public interests as opposed to narrow local interests. To date, proposals for bold state planning and action in land-use policy in New Jersey have met with only limited success, except for the Hackensack Meadowlands and certain phases of environmental protection. The principal stumbling block has been the home rule issue. Having once delegated most of its authority in land-use regulation to municipal government, the state is regarded as a usurper and intruder when it seeks to regain selected aspects of such powers and is looked upon as dictatorial when it seeks to establish modest standards for, or to exercise supervision over, municipal land-use decision-making processes.[6]

New Jersey's proposed comprehensive land-use planning and development act of 1969 was an effort to strengthen the state's planning role by establishing an interagency state planning commission, which was to be charged with (1) recommending a long-range capital improvements program coordinating state agency capital requirements; (2) delineating critical areas around selected state and federal installations; (3) recommending state purchases of sites to be placed into a state land reserve for subsequent state use; and (4) recommending state acquisition of sites for new communities to be disposed of under long-term lease (or other terms) to private sponsors.[7] The proposed legislation attempted to avoid a direct confrontation with the home rule controversy by making no provision for mandatory state review and approval of municipal land-use decisions.

Planning legislation proposed in 1972 represented a step forward in certain areas, including the requirement for the development of a state development plan and an official state map, but it also skirted the home rule issue. For example, state review and certification of municipal development regulations was to be purely at the option of the municipality.

Regional Impact Districts

Many states contain relatively large well-defined areas with special development problems, the boundaries and needs of which transcend the political jurisdictions and collective capabilities of municipalities and counties. Dealing with such cases usually requires special legislation to create new public agencies—agencies endowed with land-use powers ordinarily reserved to municipalities and with financial powers associated with public corporate bodies.

The Hackensack Meadowlands District, previously described in Chapter 1 in some detail, is the prime example of such a special district in New Jersey. Establishment of this district on the assumption that municipalities and counties (within whose jurisdictions the meadows belonged) had failed to exploit the development potential of the tract, represents a flank attack on the home rule principle. Furthermore, the affected municipalities and county governments were prepared to admit that there were no serious prospects on hand to ensure future development.

An example of a large special impact district with an open space orientation is the Pinelands region, a 950-acre area located in southeast central New Jersey. Traditionally lightly settled and used for agriculture, the area has been shifting increasingly to recreational purposes. Plans for large-scale urbanization of portions of this area emerged periodically during the 20th century, but all proposals, including plans for a massive jetport, proved abortive. Partly in response to these proposals, New Jersey adopted legislation aimed at protecting the Pinelands. This legislation has a number of purposes, including "the protection of the water resources and other natural assets of the Pinelands region from misuse and pollution; the conservation of the scientific, educational, and scenic water resources and the recreational values of the region; the encouragement of the continuation and development of compatible land uses in order to improve the over-all environmental and economic position of the area; and the presentation and promotion of the agricultural complex of the Pinelands regions."[8] To carry out these purposes, the legislation created a 15-member Pinelands Environmental Council, the majority of whom are county freeholders or mayors of the two counties in which the region is located. The council's major responsibility is to develop a "coordinative, comprehensive plan"; and to "encourage and assist public and private agencies and persons to undertake projects and activities in accordance with the coordinative, comprehensive plan."[9]

The Pinelands Environmental Council represents a good illustration of a regional governmental body whose powers are largely limited to mandatory referral and review. Under terms of this legislation, procedures are outlined for preliminary consultation with the Council about any proposed projects and for final Council review of such projects. Although projects that would "destroy or substantially impair significant historic or recreational resources or bring about a major change in the appearance or use of an area of the Pinelands region'' are subject to review under the act, the powers of the Council are restricted to delaying orders through further review and public hearings.[10] Outside of persuasive pressures generated by such public hearings and the dissemination of Council findings, the Council's principal instrument to deter development deemed unfavorable is to transmit its reports to public agencies that have the power to review or approve proposed projects. Therefore the council represents only a slight infringement on the home rule principle in land-use regulation.

A regional impact mechanism with far greater authority to guide and control development is authorized by the Coastal Facility Review Act of 1973.[11] An effort to protect New Jersey's extensive coastal areas and the land bordering the Delaware River, this legislation established a system of licensing, under the control of the State Commissioner of Environmental Protection, based on environmental impact statements and information presented at public hearings. The legislation identifies a broad range of facilities deemed to have possible adverse economic, social, and aesthetic impacts on the state. These include electric power generation; food and food byproducts; incineration wastes; paper production; public facilities and housing, including sanitary landfills, waste treatment plants, road, airport, or highway construction, new housing developments of 25 or more dwellings, and expansion of existing housing developments by the addition of 25 or more dwelling units; agrichemical production; inorganic acids and salts manufacture; mineral products; chemical processes; storage; metallurgical processes; and so on. This legislation represents an attempt to make the state take a more active role in protecting a critical zone, one that had already suffered serious exploitation under the traditional patchwork of land-use controls. Since the act goes well beyond mandatory referral and review to a licensing system that covers a wide range of development activities, it was successfully opposed by a coalition of affected industries and some trade unions in 1972 and the spring of 1973. Under strong gubernatorial pressure, however, a revised version of this legislation, which somewhat reduced the geographic area subject to control and restricted the legislation's coverage to new facilities, was enacted during a special session called in June 1973. The State Department of Environmental Protection, the prime implementation agency under the act, has been engaged in an extensive resource inventory and mapping program to provide the data base needed for carrying out its responsibilities under the legislation.

Role of the Federal Government

The recognition that further national urban growth was inevitable and that, in view of past disasters, such growth should be better focused and planned led to the passage in 1970 of Title VII of the Housing and Urban Development Act. The act provided for grants and loans to assist the planning and financing of new communities in town and in outlying areas that met specified land-use criteria. The term "land use" was interpreted broadly to include environmental and social criteria. In addition, the legislation encouraged the introduction of innovative technology. Thus the federal government, which does not have police powers affecting land use, has enacted legislation combining substantial financial incentives and rigorous review to improve the quality of new urban development. Under this approach, however, the federal government remains in a relatively passive respondent role, acting only upon the initiatives of private developers and lower-level governments.

Alternative Methods of Allocating Governmental Responsibilities

Once it is conceded that the current system of fragmented municipal responsibility for land-use decisions is unsatisfactory, there are three major options available to transfer land-use decision-making power from local to higher levels of government:

1. Review and approval of municipal development controls.
2. Override of local land-use controls.
3. Transfer of municipal development controls.

Review of Municipal Development Controls by
Higher Level of Government

For some years, it has been suggested that municipal land-use deci-

sions be subjected to review and approval by a higher level of
government to assure a greater degree of consistency in inter-
governmental land-use planning and programming, and to provide
some assurance that local governments would take into account a
broader public interest in making such decisions. The review process can take a variety of forms. Perhaps the mildest alternative is the
review conducted by state government solely at the request and
option of the municipality, as provided in New Jersey's 1972 proposed community planning legislation. A stronger posture was
urged in 1968 by the National Commission on Urban Problems,
which called for review and approval by appropriate state agencies
of municipal land-use regulations and decisions.

A number of states have enacted legislation requiring varying
degrees of review and approval of municipal land-use ordinances
and decisions. In Maine, the State Environmental Improvement
Commission is authorized to review and approve commercial and
industrial uses, which (a) require commission licenses; (b) which
occupy land areas in excess of 20 acres; (c) which contemplate
excavation of natural resources; (d) which occupy on a single parcel
a structure or structures with total floor areas of over 60,000 square
feet. Excluded from the review and approval process are developments by (a) public agencies; (b) the forest products industry; or
(c) the electric power industry. Residential subdivisions of over 20
acres are considered commercial developments. Among the criteria
for state evaluation of applications are the financial capacity of the
applicant to provide for antipollution measures and assurances of
protection for the natural environment and property values. Development proposals covered by the Maine legislation are presented
directly to the Environmental Improvement Commission in the form
of detailed letters of intent rather than through the municipal land-
use regulatory authorities. Thus the Maine legislation provides for
review and approval of large-scale private developments rather than
review and approval of municipal land-use regulations or
decisions.[12] Unfortunately, the implementation of this legislation
has been seriously handicapped by the assignment of minimum staff
to the administration of this important function.

A more vigorous and inclusive system of land-use regulation has
been adopted by Vermont. Under legislation passed in 1970,[13] the
state requires prospective developers to present proof that their
proposals will be environmentally sound, will not place unreason-

able burdens on public facilities and services, and are in confor-
mance with any duly adopted state or regional plan. The legislation
established a State Environmental Board charged with issuing development permits and with preparing a comprehensive land-use
plan for the state. The legislation also created seven district commis-
sions, which serve under the board to assist in screening and adjudicating development applications.

The Vermont legislation goes farther than the legislation passed
in Maine. Permits must be secured for any commercial or industrial
construction exceeding 10 acres; for housing projects containing 10
or more dwelling units within a radius of five miles, from the two
most widely separated locations; for any development over 2500 feet
in elevation; and for subdivisions of 10 or more lots. In addition, the
legislation requires municipalities and state agencies to apply for
development permits for proposed public construction. The principal exemptions from the review and approval process are the farming, forest, and electric power industries. Moreover, since the legislation is not retroactive, it permits a large volume of major construction to be undertaken without the permit process.

New York State provides another example of review of municipal development regulations by a higher-level jurisdiction. Under
legislation enacted in 1960, municipal zoning agencies within counties that have county, metropolitan, or regional planning organizations are required to refer to the latter certain proposed zoning
actions that have regional impact prior to taking final action thereon.
Regional impact matters are defined in this legislation as follows:

(a) Any municipal zoning regulation, or any amendment thereof, which
    would change the district classification of or the regulations applying to
    real property lying within a distance of five hundred feet from the
    boundary of any city, village, or town, or from the boundary of any
    county or state park or other vacation area, or from the right-of-way of
    any county or state parkway, thruway, expressway or other
    controlled-access highway or from the right-of-way of any stream or
    drainage channel owned by the county or for which the county has
    controlled channel lines, or from the boundary of any county or state
    owned land on which a public building or institution is situated;

(b) Any proposed special permit or variance affecting land or a building
    within such distance of five hundred feet.[14]

The county, metropolitan, or regional planning agency to which
such zoning regulation matters of regional impact are referred is

required within 30 days after receiving a full statement of the referred matter to report its recommendations, including a full statement of the reasons for such recommendations, to the affected municipal zoning agency. When the regional planning agency fails to report within the 30-day or longer period, as agreed upon by the parties, the municipal zoning agency may take final action without such report. When the regional planning agency disapproves the local proposal or recommends modification thereof, the municipal zoning agency may override the disapproval or recommendation only upon a majority vote of all the members of the local body and only after adopting a resolution stating the reasons for any contrary action.

Although this New York precedent does not give regional planning agencies the power to veto local zoning regulations and decisions with regional impact, the mandatory review and reporting procedure contains the useful components of early warning and further public exposure to guarantee that local land regulation agencies recognize fully the regional implications of their tentative decisions.

Override of Local Land-Use Controls by Higher Levels of Government

There are also various kinds of compromise legislation under which municipal government retains land-use control but under which the home rule principle may be overridden by the state to achieve selective, limited objectives in the broad public interest. Usually local government is given complete opportunity to revise its land-use regulations to conform to state standards. Only where there is such a failure to act does the state intervene.

One major area where state intervention has been deemed necessary is in housing for low-income families. In accordance with their local interests, municipalities normally prefer to bar the door to such housing. State government, therefore, considers it necessary to force municipalities to accept a "fair share" of the region's needs for such housing units. The 1968 Kaiser Committee report recommended that the United States Department of Housing and Urban Development (HUD) be given the power to override municipal deterrents to the construction of low-income housing.[15] In practice,

HUD adopted such a posture through administrative regulations that required communities to accept proposals for such housing on penalty of losing pending federal grants for sewers, water, and housing for the elderly. Subsequently, however, HUD released its pressure on communities by ceasing to link approval of federal public facility grants with favorable local action on proposals for housing low-income families.

With the withdrawal of federal leverage from the equation, the exercise of leadership to generate changes in municipal land-use regulations relevant to this type of housing shifted to the states. A notable example of state intervention to achieve broad housing goals was the State Urban Development Corporation (UDC), which was created by New York in 1968.[16] Among its other powers and functions, the UDC was given the authority to override local zoning ordinances and building codes. After operating for several years by using this overriding device sparingly, while threatening its application if municipalities did not accept "a fair share" of housing for low-income families, the UDC ran afoul of powerful local resistance from communities in Westchester County. In 1973, the state legislature stripped the UDC of its power to preempt local zoning and building codes in towns and villages. However, the override power is retained with respect to cities.

Massachusetts legislation adopted in 1969 was specifically designed to achieve housing objectives similar to those in New York State.[17] The Massachusetts statute, widely known as the "anti-snob" zoning law, prescribed a quota of housing for low- and moderate-income housing for each municipality in the state. The maximum amount of such housing that a community need accept was established at 10 percent of the total number of housing units it contained as reported in the latest census. The statute established a zoning appeals committee in the State Department of Community Affairs (DCA), which was empowered to overrule local zoning decisions rejecting proposals for housing low-income families. As might be expected, strong suburban resistance was encountered when DCA attempted to exercise its power to override local decisions. Early in 1973, the Massachusetts Supreme Judicial Court upheld the constitutionality of the statute in suits brought by the board of appeals of two suburban communities.[18] In ruling that the municipality's power to control its land use by zoning regulations is not unlimited, the court reiterated its 1942 opinion in *Simon* v. *Needham* (311 Mass. 560, 565-66):

A zoning by-law cannot be adopted for the purpose of setting up a barrier against the influx of thrifty and respectable citizens who desire to live there and who are able and willing to erect homes on lots upon which fair and reasonable restrictions have been imposed, not for the purpose of protecting the large estates that are already located in the district. The strictly local interests of the town must yield if it appears that they are plainly in conflict with the general interests of the public at large, and in such instances the interest of the municipality would not be allowed to stand in the way.[19]

Under the Massachusetts statute, the developer whose housing proposal has been rejected by the local board of appeals must present proof to the DCA appeals committee that the local denial was not "reasonable and consistent with local needs." One prominent planner had felt that this provision requiring consistency with local needs was one of the weaker elements of the legislation.[20] The opinion of the Massachusetts Supreme Judicial Court, however, removed this doubt since it clearly stipulated that the legislature's 10 percent quota was a reasonable requirement for municipalities to meet if regional housing goals were to be achieved.

The decision of the Supreme Judicial Court had an almost immediate impact. In August 1973, the DCA appeals committee approved the construction of 600 units of housing for low- and moderate-income families, overruling local objections revolving around possible water shortages and potentially dangerous drainage conditions. Moreover, this action in three suburban communities by the appeals committee was believed to pave the way for similar approval of an additional 1075 housing units in four other suburban communities. However, as a result of a variety of circumstances, including the federal moratorium on HUD housing subsidies that began in 1973 and rapid and substantial increases in construction costs, little in the way of tangible results is visible.

Kentucky provides an example of a modest effort in the intervention of higher levels of government to stimulate local communities to enter into cooperative planning units that coincide more reasonably with the scale of current urban needs and problems. A key provision of the Kentucky legislation grants power to the county to require municipal government to enter into joint planning arrangements unless they can demonstrate that they have been unsuccessful in their attempts to do so.[21]

Another limited example of the intervention of higher governmental jurisdictions to mandate local land-use regulation can be found in Wisconsin. Legislation passed in 1965 requires counties to protect lakefront, shorelines, and river flood plains through the enactment of zoning ordinances. In instances where counties fail to comply with adopting ordinances satisfactory to the State Department of Natural Resources, the state is empowered to impose and enforce a state drafted ordinance. In theory, it has been suggested, this approach might be used to require municipalities and counties to adopt land-use controls for the protection of other critical areas.[22]

In practice, the Wisconsin legislation has demonstrated a number of serious deficiencies. The state has no power to insure the enforcement of the state-mandated ordinance. Nor does it have the power to review the exceptions that the counties may grant. Finally, it has no assurance that counties have the requisite technical staff to delineate flood plains. For these reasons, county adoptions of flood plain regulatory ordinances have proved to be only *pro forma* exercises in which the county officially accedes to state imposed criteria but makes no real effort to alter its previous land-use practices.

Transfer of Development Controls to Higher Levels
of Government

The most extreme alternative for allocating governmental responsibility in land-use control is the outright transfer of such powers to a higher jurisdiction, a process that amounts to a dismantling of the home rule principle in this area. In 1968, the National Commission on Urban Problems adopted this approach by recommending that counties or regional governments exercise exclusive land-use controls in the smaller cities of metropolitan areas (under 25,000 population and four square miles in area).[23] In most states, however, counties tend to be weak, perhaps atrophied governmental units, and metropolitan government remains an unattained objective. The few metropolitan governments that do exist tend to be federations rather than unitary bodies, and land-use controls continue to be a municipal responsibility.

From time to time, proposals for metropolitan solutions are advanced that would transfer substantial land-use regulatory powers to the metropolitan level. In Massachusetts, for example, legislation was introduced in 1973 calling for the establishment of a Metropolitan Council, which, among other powers, would be given responsibility for preparing a comprehensive development plan subject to the guidelines, policies, and standards of the state's land-use planning agency, including the adoption of rules and regulations concerning the land-use concerns and areas enumerated below:

1. The use and development of areas of critical environmental concern, that is, areas where uncontrolled or incompatible development could result in damage to the environment, life, or property or the long-term public interest which is of more than local significance.
2. The use of land within areas which are or may be impacted by key facilities, that is, public facilities which tend to induce development and urbanization of more than local impact.
3. Local regulations which may arbitrarily or capriciously restrict or exclude development of public facilities or utilities of regional benefit.
4. The location of new communities and the use of land around new communities.
5. Development of regional impact, that is, any development which, because of its character, magnitude, or location would have a substantial effect upon the health, safety, or welfare of citizens of more than one municipality.[24]

The only example of outright assumption of land-use control powers at a higher level of government in the nation is in Hawaii. The Hawaiian approach is consistent with the high degree of centralization that characterizes major areas of governmental activity in that state, including state-operated and financed public schools. As previously noted in this report, Hawaii's policy of state land-use controls is closely linked to its property taxation policies.

The State Land Use Commission classifies all land in the state into four major land-use categories or districts: urban, rural, agricultural, and conservation. As was mentioned in Chapter 4, in urban districts, land is still subject to local zoning. Planning and zoning are administered by the counties in all but the conservation districts, the uses of which are controlled by the state.[25] The State Land Use Commission (LUC) is an unsalaried body of nine members limited in staff assistance to an administrator and a planner. The LUC is also assisted to some degree by the staff of the state planning agency.

The LUC has delineated sufficient land within urban districts to satisfy 10 years of projected urban expansion. Developers who wish to build on agricultural land must show why they cannot build on existing urban district land. The LUC determines what uses can be permitted in the agricultural districts, although counties can permit other uses by special permit. Development in conservation districts is governed by a State Board of Land and Natural Resources, which also has a limited staff.

The LUC is required to redistrict land every five years, based on three criteria:

1. Prime agricultural land should be preserved.
2. The tourist industry should be developed without injuring the natural landscape.
3. Compact efficient urban areas should be developed where people may live at reasonable cost.

The Hawaiian approach has been criticized on two principal grounds:

1. It has been alleged that the policy of channeling growth into relatively small areas is driving up the already high price of sites suitable for development.
2. The State Land Use Commission has not yet prepared an up-to-date use plan and is using the state's 1969 plan as its guide.

In addition to the above major criticisms, Hawaii's approach to land-use controls has been attacked for failure of the taxation agencies to base their decisions on the LUC's land classifications. Moreover, it is charged that the LUC's lack of staff renders it incapable of effective implementation of land-use planning.

Another approach to state land-use planning was adopted by Florida. Florida's Environmental Land and Water Management Act of 1972 follows the guidelines recommended by the model land-development code of the American Law Institute. The Act established a state land planning agency within the state planning agency. The land planning agency is charged with two major responsibilities:

1. To make recommendations on designated critical areas. (The law limits such critical areas to a maximum of 5 percent of the state.)
2. To recommend development guidelines in critical areas and for developments with regional impact anywhere in the state.

In practice, the Governor and Cabinet are actually the land

planning agency, designating critical areas and issuing development guidelines. The Governor and Cabinet also make up the land and water adjudicatory commission, which acts as an appeals board. The act provides for judicial review in decisions contested on constitutional grounds.

One interesting feature of the legislation is the provision for a 15 member environmental land management study committee, which includes representation from the academic community and from environmental groups.[26] This breadth of representation and the focus on gubernatorial leadership in the Act may be worthy of emulation.

This analysis of alternative methods of allocating governmental responsibility for land-use regulation indicates that there are no clear-cut, universally valid models for New Jersey to adopt. It is evident that while New Jersey may be able to adapt legislative approaches proposed or adopted in other states, it remains necessary for the state to evolve a jurisdictional arrangement for land-use regulation tailored to its special needs and traditions. The form and substance of such a system is discussed in the final chapter.

7

Summary and Evaluation of the Techniques of Land-Use Controls

Introduction: Alternate Techniques of Land-Use Regulation

The history of American land-use policy has been a history of land *development*.[a] From the Northwest Ordinance of 1787 to the Homestead Act of 1862 to the large scale FHA mortgage insurance programs in aid of home ownership after World War II, the objective of land-use policy has been the development of land to meet the shifting patterns of national migration and urbanization trends. During the nineteenth century, opportunities for land ownership and development were used to accelerate migration to the Western states. During the last half of the nineteenth century, intensive land development was encouraged to provide for the aggregations of population in the cities. In the middle of the twentieth century, national housing and transportation policies encouraged the development of land to create suburban communities around those cities. Currently, a new migration of population appears to be shifting from metropolitan areas to outlying areas.[1] Increasing affluence, leisure-oriented life styles encouraged by manufacturers of second homes, the desire to move away from core city problems, the recreation hotel-motel industry, the road builders,[2] as well as the real estate developers, have created a surge of demand for land development beyond the regulating ability of existing techniques of land-use control.

In view of rising concerns over energy shortages and particularly the increasing costs of motor fuel, some of the demand for widely dispersed types of development may be diminished in favor of a trend toward nodal urban development, which can be facilitated by improved public transportation. This may imply that public policy must renew its attention to the land-use development uses in the older urban areas, many of which have essentially been written off.

---

[a]Two notable exceptions to this generalization are the Conservation Movement during the administration of Theodore Roosevelt and the Greenbelt Movement during the administration of Franklin Delano Roosevelt

83

In addition, land-development problems may increasingly confront the suburban and outlying communities, which are available for high-density or intensive development.

An examination of existing techniques of regulating land development is useful to determine the limits of effectiveness of those techniques.[3] Some techniques are in general use; others are proposals that have not been widely adopted. Considered together, the following constitute the current legal approaches to land-use controls: (1) police power regulation (for example, zoning and subdivision control); (2) eminent domain, including public acquisition of the fee, compensable regulation, and public acquisition of less than the fee (for example, conservation easements); and (3) taxation.

Advantages and Disadvantages of Alternate Techniques

Police Power Regulation

Police power regulation is based upon the principle that in a society governed by law everyone must submit to reasonable regulation of his liberty and property to prevent the abuse of these rights by those who are unskillful, careless, or unscrupulous.[4] The police power is exercised by government "to promote and protect the health, safety morals, comfort and general welfare of the people."[5] Based upon this power, states have delegated to local government the power to regulate the use of property and "to impair the owner's rights therein to some *reasonable extent* without compensation because the Legislature, acting under the police power of the state, deems the free exercise of such rights detrimental to the public interests"[6] (emphasis added). Municipalities meet this responsibility under police power regulation through planning, zoning, subdivision control, official maps, and building and housing codes. Moreover, police power can also be used to assure the setting aside and preservation of limited amounts of open space through minimum requirements and incentives incorporated in zoning, subdivision control, and official map regulations.

As noted in Chapter 2, each category of police power has certain strengths and weaknesses. The application of municipal and regional planning, for example, provides orderly, predictable, and rational directions for land-use development and can be helpful in conserving property values and natural amenities. However, planning tends to be a weak advisory function outside the mainstream of decision making. Like planning, zoning assists communities in developing and preserving predictable and goal-oriented land-development patterns. Where planning has been criticized for being too weak, zoning has been faulted for being too rigid. The result has been land-use management by exception through the frequent granting of variances. In addition, both planning and zoning have been blamed for producing sterile, segregated land-use development patterns, partly through an excessive focus on parcel-by-parcel development. Another major weakness of municipal planning and zoning is the failure to take into account intermunicipal land-use relationships and dependencies. This has necessitated adjudication at higher levels of authority, including the courts. To a degree, the failure to consider intermunicipal linkages is related to competitive land-use practices, such as fiscal and exclusionary zoning, in which municipalities seek to attract net tax generators and to exclude uses that impose substantial municipal social and economic costs.

Another major form of police power, subdivision control, has advantages similar to those for planning and zoning in that it provides reasonable assurances of stable, orderly development. In addition, it can be used to guarantee the installation and quality of utilities and other elements of the basic infrastructure, as well as to provide limited amounts of open space. In practice, however, subdivision control falls short of its potential since the process has not been adequately connected to effective site design review. In addition, subdivision control tends to be a single step rather than a continuing review process for guiding land-use development.

Planned Unit Developments represent a considerable improvement over traditional planning, zoning, and subdivision control practices. PUD's provide development at substantial scale, which can be held to high design requirements and environmental controls, while providing flexibility and diversity in land use. Principal weaknesses of the PUD approach lie in the failure to take adequate account of the impacts on areas outside and adjacent to the PUD and the failure to require neighboring municipalities to weave the substantial development represented by a PUD into the fabric of their planning and zoning programs. Moreover, the development of a

PUD does not of itself provide any guarantee that its residents will include a broad spectrum of social and economic classes.

The difficulty in relying upon the police power to preserve open space lies in the lack of objective standards for determining whether the property-use restriction is reasonable under the circumstances.[7] In determining the "reasonableness" (and therefore the validity) of a land-use regulation, a court must weigh the evidence relating to the public interest and the rights of the property owner. As a result of this comparative evaluation, the court may determine that the public interest is so slight or the deprivation of the owner is so great that the regulation is "unreasonable" under the circumstances and, therefore, invalid as a violation of substantive due process.[8] Based upon this reasoning, courts have held invalid zoning ordinances restricting land use to flood storage and open space,[9] parking lot purposes,[10] school and recreational use,[11] and greenbelt and park purposes.[12] Similarly, subdivision regulations have been held invalid, in spite of a substantial public interest, where the owner is denied reasonable use of his property.[13]

In *Morris County Land Improvement Co.* v. *Parsippany-Troy Hills Township*,[14] a leading case on the issue of zoning regulation for flood detention purposes, the court conceded that the determination of whether the ordinance is a valid regulation or an invalid taking is always a matter of degree, but stated that "there is no question that the line has been crossed when the purpose and practical effect of the regulation is to appropriate private property for a floodwater basin or open space."[15] The court stated that public *acquisition* (with compensation) rather than *regulation* (without compensation) was required to provide land for open space. To the extent that this principle continues to be adopted by the courts, police power regulation will not provide an effective technique for preserving open space.

Eminent Domain

An important tool for controlling land-use development is eminent domain. As noted in Chapter 3, eminent domain is the power to acquire land needed for public purposes upon payment of reasonable compensation to the owner. Two major applications of eminent domain power are (1) open space acquisition programs; and (2) the urban renewal program, under which public takings are made in designated blighted urban areas for planned redevelopment.

The power of the federal and state governments to acquire property for park and recreational purposes is well-established.[16] A number of states, including New Jersey,[17] New York,[18] Massachusetts,[19] California,[20] and Wisconsin[21] have authorized state or local government acquisition of land for recreational, conservation, or open space purposes. There is little doubt about the effectiveness of this technique to preserve open space—when it can be implemented. The primary impediment to the use of public acquisition of the fee is the lack of funds available for this purpose. Voter reluctance to approve programs or bond issues that will result in increased taxation is a serious obstacle. The numerous federal programs of financial assistance for local government acquisition of land[22] have not overcome this problem because the federal appropriations under these programs can fill only a very small proportion of the need.

In addition to the lack of financial resources, there are other objections to the public acquisition of lands for open space preservation:

1. When title is transferred from private to public ownership, the property is removed from the tax rolls and the remaining property owners in the jurisdiction must bear a proportionately larger share of the tax burden.
2. There exists in many areas of the nation strong political opposition to government ownership and management of land.
3. Many farmers and other landowners are unwilling to relinquish possession of their land even for a fair consideration.
4. Although preservation of open space is a commendable objective, the high costs of land acquisition may divert substantial public resources from other objectives deemed to have a higher priority, such as education and housing.

Taken together these factors have created a formidable obstacle to the widespread use of public acquisition of land for open space preservation.

Compensable Regulation. To overcome the constitutional objection to the harsh effect of depriving an owner of the use of his property if it is restricted to open space purposes, as discussed in Chapter 4,

Krasnowiecki and Paul proposed a system by which owners would be compensated for part of their losses.[23] Under their proposal, an owner would be compensated for the loss of the development value of his property at the time the controls were imposed. For example, an owner of agricultural land with a market value of $1000 before it is restricted to open space use would be entitled to compensation of $400 if the market value of his land is reduced to only $600 when restricted to agricultural or other open space use. The proposed compensation represents the development value of the property "taken" from the owner by the police power restriction upon the use of his property. The owner would not be eligible for compensation until he sells the property because, until such sale, he would have not incurred any loss. To prevent fraudulent claims for excessive compensation, the proposal includes a requirement for an administratively controlled public sale.

The Krasnowiecki and Paul proposal is based upon a skillful and imaginative combination of the police power and the eminent domain power. The harshness of police power restriction is softened by compensation for the loss of the development value at the time of regulation. In spite of these advantages, compensable regulation has not been utilized as an effective technique for preserving open space for a number of reasons. The primary reason is that the American public does not seem prepared to accept a program that denies a property owner the speculative value of his property, that is, the value based upon an expectation, whether real or fancied, that the value will continue to increase with time. Second, the public and the legal profession are not sufficiently comfortable with the concept of development rights and are fearful of unknown consequences of the concept upon the real estate market. Third, the proposal requires a relatively complex system of governmental administration that would tend to impede the alienability of property. Consequently, the effectiveness of compensable regulation as a technique for preserving open space remains untested.

Public Acquisition of Less Than the Fee: Conservation Easements. As previously noted, in 1959 William H. Whyte, Jr. proposed a method of preserving open space by authorizing governments to acquire only the owner's right to develop the land, leaving him with all other rights of ownership including the right of continued possession.[24] Whyte called this right a "conservation easement" because the purpose of such acquisition by government is to conserve environmental amenities such as land, air, soil, open space, and historic areas. After acquisition of the conservation easement by the government, the owner continues to own and use his land, subject only to the right of the government to prevent its development. The easement runs with the land and binds all subsequent purchases.

Public acquisition of the conservation easement rather than the fee simple (entire title) has a number of advantages:

1. The cost of acquisition of a conservation easement is less than the cost of the fee simple. The value of a conservation easement would be the difference between the value of the land without any restriction on development and the value of the land restricted to agricultural or other open space uses. Consequently, in rural areas, outside the influence of demand for urban development, the conservation easement could be acquired at very low cost.

2. There would be less opposition from farmers to the acquisition of conservation easements because they would be able to remain in possession and use their land for farming purposes.

3. The land would remain on the tax rolls and at the time of acquisition would not impose any appreciable burden upon other property owners. The property tax would be imposed upon the assessed value of the land restricted to agricultural or open space use. Therefore, property taxes would not increase as development values rise and would not make the land too costly to maintain for farming purposes. As the demand for development in the area increases, the owners of developable land would reap the benefits of increased value and would pay taxes upon a higher assessed value.

In spite of these apparent advantages, public acquisition of conservation easements has not been an effective technique of preserving open space. As one critic put it, "a policy of taking conservation easements is undesirable, potentially unfair, and legally dangerous."[25] It has been argued that conservation easements are not effective where they are used to make significant changes in existing land use or where real estate speculation has affected the market value of the land.[26] Because of such difficulties, the National Park Service discontinued the acquisition of scenic easements and reported: "On the basis of 20 years of experience, such easements breed misunderstandings, administrative difficulties, are difficult to enforce, and cost only a little less than the fee."[27]

Thus it seems clear that each of the existing techniques of preserving open space has one or more serious limitations that make it incapable of preventing the development of land in the amount and locations necessary to enhance the quality of life in metropolitan areas. New and imaginative techniques must be devised, refined, and perfected for this purpose. The separation and marketability of development rights may provide the legal instrumentality by which open space may be preserved in a manner that is consistent with constitutionally protected property rights and the realities of municipal finance.

Urban Renewal. The urban renewal approach has several major advantages. First, it provides the only feasible legal avenue whereby eminent domain power is used to encourage private land development. Second, federal and state subsidies available through the urban renewal program make possible the land assembly needed for redeveloping built-up urban areas and for offsetting the difference in cost between property takings and sale of land to developers. Finally, the urban renewal program requires, to a substantial degree, sophisticated comprehensive planning along with a potentially useful design review process.

The urban renewal approach has suffered from a number of disadvantages. The emphasis on economic viability and tax returns from projects has tended to subordinate the housing goals of low- and moderate-income families. While nonresidential re-uses under urban renewal have resulted in substantial achievements at relatively high costs, with respect to residential areas, the results have been mixed. In some cases, urban renewal subsidies have been used to construct housing benefitting affluent families and developers. In other cases, housing developments in urban renewal areas for low-income families have demonstrated that improvements in portions of the physical environment cannot compensate for general economic and social disadvantages, which include high unemployment, lack of marketable skills, and excessive crime rates.

Taxation Policies

Taxation policies are primarily designed to generate revenues to support public services. At the municipal level, most revenues are derived from ad valorem taxes on land and buildings, and taxation policies are aimed at maximizing tax yield. The land-use and land-development impacts of municipal tax policies are extremely powerful, but they have tended to be viewed mainly in fiscal terms rather than in their implications for land use and development.

Alleged advantages of property taxation include ease of collection and comprehensiveness of coverage (property owners cannot conceal their assets from local assessors) and the sociopolitical value of developing a direct linkage between residence, property ownership, and municipal expenditures and services. Municipal tax policies have been criticized as engendering and perpetuating wide tax base disparities among communities and for fostering competitive fiscal zoning aimed at maximizing local revenues (often to the disadvantage of other communities). In addition, fair assessment for tax purposes is often difficult to achieve in practice and there are continuing charges of tax discrimination and favoritism. Property taxes are highly regressive since they tend to get passed on to renters in the form of a relatively high kind of sales tax. Finally, property taxation policies tend to reward speculators who "milk" their property, to penalize investors interested in sound orderly development, and to encourage the development of the dwindling supply of open land to generate municipal tax revenues.

Implementation and Use of Recommended Techniques of Land-Use Controls

The final chapter of this report, entitled "Conclusions and Recommendations," presents in some detail a proposed program of land-use controls specifically applicable to land-use problems surrounding PUD's in New Jersey, but it also includes recommendations to strengthen state, regional, and municipal land-use development policies.

In summary, it is recommended that police power regulation in land use be made more effective by:

1. Adopting a New Jersey state enabling act updating and modernizing all major aspects of municipal and regional controls in land-use development—it should include the areas of municipal planning powers, processes, and organization; master planning and capital improvements programming, including project review; the official map; subdivision regulation; site plan review; zoning; inter-

municipal and regional planning arrangements; and county planning powers, processes, and organization.

2. Incorporated within this new state enabling act should be the following innovative techniques for police power regulation in land-use development: (a) incentive zoning and (b) expansion of environmental impact controls. This report has weighed the pros and cons of a variety of land-use control techniques under police power regulation and has concluded that two are not suitable for New Jersey because of uncertainties surrounding their legality under existing state law: these two are floating zones and contract zoning. A third, controlled sequential development, while upheld in the *Ramapo* case (discussed in detail in Chapter 2), has potential as a device for guiding orderly development but must be carefully monitored lest it become a new device for implementing exclusionary goals. While the concept of performance zoning applied to industrial zoning classifications is attractive, it has proved to be extremely difficult to administer. It is therefore not recommended for adoption.

The major proposal under the heading of eminent domain calls for (a) New Jersey legislation that will authorize the state regional development authorities and municipalities to establish land banks for acquiring and holding land needed for future development (as sites for public facilities and as tracts for planned private development); and (b) legislation that will authorize experimentation with development rights to encourage the preservation of open space at minimum cost and to assist in guiding orderly development.

3. In the sphere of taxation policy, the final chapter recommends that (a) the state reduce excessive reliance on local property taxes by assuming fiscal responsibility for such services as education, welfare, and the administration of justice; (b) a limited experimental program in site value taxation for cities over 100,000 population be implemented; and (c) an examination be initiated of adapting the land-use taxation experience of Hawaii and Vermont to New Jersey.

Not recommended as a solution to the property tax dilemma is a system of property tax classification, such as has been adopted in Minnesota and Montana, because abandoning uniformity seems to create as many tax inequities and injustices as it removes.

A major thesis of this report is that extramunicipal powers are indispensable to a rational effective system of land-use control. Strengthening municipal powers and processes in land-use regulation would certainly be helpful, but it alone would not be sufficient to deal with intermunicipal and regional problems, such as those posed by PUD's and new communities. These substantial development issues cannot be dealt with effectively at the county or regional level, partly because of the inherent weaknesses of county government and the extreme political difficulty involved in creating strong broad-purpose regional governmental authorities. For this reason, we have focused major attention on the leadership and planning role of state government.

In summary, we propose establishment of a State Land Use Resources Commission to prepare a state land-use plan and to recommend an appropriate state implementing mechanism, with supporting regional planning districts, possibly on the Vermont model. In addition, our recommendations call for a stronger version of those sections of the proposed 1972 Community Planning Law that pertain to state planning and development. The major change suggested is to make state review of the land-use regulations and plans of municipalities and private developers mandatory (as would be the case with developments in critical areas), rather than permissive.

Finally, we recommend that the state take the lead in devising and implementing a "fair share" housing policy to make the suburbs more accessible to low- and moderate-income families. This has emerged as an inescapable responsibility in light of a series of court decisions in New Jersey and elsewhere aimed at existing exclusionary land-use practices.

8 Conclusions and Recommendations

Introduction

As noted from time to time in this study, its primary concern—the land-use impacts on areas adjoining PUDs and new communities—is a subject that is intimately bound up with state, county, and municipal land-use regulation systems. For this reason, the previous chapters of this report ranged over a broad spectrum of existing and proposed approaches for guiding and controlling development in various states that have taken a leading role in this field, including New Jersey. Prior chapters also reviewed existing and alternative systems for allocating public responsibilities in carrying out land-use regulation powers. A major conclusion, documented in the text, is that a fully effective system of controls over land surrounding PUDs and new communities requires a thorough revamping of state land-use policies and mechanisms.

This chapter contains an outline of recommendations for an appropriate state posture in the area of land-use development and regulation. As indicated by the foregoing analysis, no single state has in operation a completely effective model suitable for adoption in New Jersey. Nor is there a single tool or approach that promises to resolve the many complex issues and problems linked to the control and allocation of land uses.

The need for action on the part of New Jersey is rendered increasingly urgent, not only by the existence of manifold critical unresolved land-use issues, but by national land-use legislation that may offer major incentives to the states to assume leadership in effective land-use planning. Proposed federal land-use legislation failed to pass in 1973, but similar legislation to be introduced in the 1974-1975 session would assist the states in establishing a statewide planning process and in setting up and administering a state land-use program. Key provisions of the bill require that such land-use programs oversee and control development in three areas to insure that:

1. The use and development of land in areas of critical environmen-

tal concern within the State is not inconsistent with the State land use program.

2. The use of land in areas within the State which are or may be impacted by key facilities . . . is not inconsistent with the State land use program.

3. Any large-scale subdivisions and other proposed large-scale development within the State of more than local significance in its impact upon the environment is not inconsistent with the State land use program.[1]

However limited and imperfect, experience in other states suggests that certain prerequisites for an effective land-use planning and management system can be identified. These include:

1. An appropriate legislative mandate.

2. Preparation of sound, up-to-date land-use and related plans (statewide, functional, regional, and local), that give proper consideration to economic, social, and environmental factors.

3. The establishment of an effective land-use planning and management system that is publicly accountable, adequately empowered, of unimpeachable integrity and commanding wide public respect, and properly staffed and financed.

4. Development and maintenance of a comprehensive land-use inventory, including a data base and mapping system that includes information on natural resources, demographic factors, changing patterns of urban development, and land-use markets.

The State's leadership role in this land-use planning and management system must include:

1. Methods for coordinating the activities of state agencies that have a significant effect on land use to render them consistent with the objectives set forth in state land-use plans.

2. Direct state regulation of land use in designated critical areas.

3. State review and approval of local land-use ordinances and decisions in certain categories of development.

Tailoring General Criteria to the Special Case of New Jersey

The previous review of exemplary state land-use legislation and regulatory programs indicates that most of the states that have taken leadership in this field are only partially urbanized and are located away from the main historic area of urban development—the urbanized northeastern zone. The northeast section of the nation urbanized first and experienced the major waves of both foreign and domestic immigration. And the northeast experienced the serious degradation, congestion, and pollution that served as a warning for the progressive, less-urbanized states. In a sense, therefore, New Jersey, along with other states in this part of the country, has furnished a negative model, a preview of the unpleasant consequences of not adopting an adequate system of land-use control, a system that anticipates and shapes rather than succumbs to urban pressures.

In many respects, New Jersey is the victim of circumstances beyond its control. As pointed out on numerous occasions, New Jersey is a corridor lacking a central urban focus. The state provides the equivalent of a workshop, storage shed, dumping ground, and dormitory for the two metropolitan areas to the northeast and southwest. This combination of location and historical role has apparently led to the pervasive feeling of fatalism, of being subject to powerful forces beyond the control of state government.

Partly as a result of the recognition of personal inability to master the powerful forces infringing on its territory, an unusually strong sense of privatism has emerged in the state, that focuses on the protection of one's immediate environs and is exemplified by a powerful support for home rule. In the face of the flood tide of development streaming into the state, individual neighborhoods and communities have been attempting to maintain their traditions, homogeneity, and integrity behind the ramparts of local land-use regulations.

The development of a coherent land-use pattern in New Jersey is rendered all the more difficult by the existence of 567 independent municipalities. The fact that these municipalities are theoretically subject to a certain amount of guidance from 21 counties has had little practical impact because of the inherent legal, administrative, and financial weaknesses of county government.

That New Jersey is the most densely populated state in the nation poses a special challenge to the creation of a system responsive to real problems in development. While much of the state is still open and can therefore benefit considerably from the land-use experience of less developed states, New Jersey has the inescapable responsibility for undoing and repairing the ravages of past development errors, in its older cities, along its coastline, and along its highways. Analysis of the special nature of the task leads to the conclusion that New Jersey must adopt a bipartite land-use policy that embraces measures aimed at the redevelopment of built-up areas, as well as the protection of its remaining open spaces.

Examination of experience in New Jersey and other states indicates that the following list of certain difficult lessons can be utilized to provide guidance in shaping New Jersey's land-use system and policies.

1. *The state should retrieve selected delegated or abdicated land-use powers and responsibilities from municipalities.* Every state that has attempted to assume a position of leadership in the land-use field has found that an initial prerequisite is to regain from its municipalities some of its previously delegated land-use powers. These include land-use decisions of broad regional interest (including PUDs, new communities, major industrial parks, and public facilities). In addition, some of the traditional, less-spectacular land-use controls exercised by municipalities require state supervision and state standards. Large-lot zoning, for example, has been challenged by court decisions in New Jersey that seek to remove exclusionary barriers to housing for low-income families. As previously noted, Massachusetts has enacted a state land-use policy imposing, in effect, suburban quotas for the housing of low- and moderate-income families. The trend of events clearly suggests that state land-use policies must include a review of local land-use regulations and the imposition of standards that assess local development plans in land use, housing, and related matters, within the context of regional and state land-use plans.

2. *Experience indicates that the State cannot rely on the counties as a viable regional mechanism for land-use control.* In a number of states, most notably Hawaii and Wisconsin, there have been attempts to assign major land-use responsibilities to the county level of government. These are states in which counties have traditionally played a strong role, as contrasted with New Jersey. Even in Wisconsin, however, the reliance on county government has proved to be ineffective. As noted earlier, Wisconsin's counties tended to adopt on a *pro forma* basis regulations as required by the state government but, in practice, the counties failed to assemble the

requisite technical expertise or to alter previous land-use practices. In New Jersey, where county governments have traditionally been weak and where major reforms have proved slow and ineffective, the county cannot be considered an appropriate instrument for land-use control.

3. Metropolitanism is not a useful alternative for land-use control and supervision in New Jersey. Most of New Jersey's cities are on the fringes of the metropolitan areas of New York and Philadelphia. This fact suggests that a metropolitan approach to land-use planning similar to that operating in Minneapolis-St. Paul and recently proposed for the greater Boston area poses difficult problems. While state and regional policy must take into account the needs and impacts of the two massive metropolitan concentrations, the greater part of which are located outside of New Jersey borders, short of abdicating any coherent state policy, New Jersey cannot permit its land-use policies to be guided by other sovereign states or metropolitan areas located primarily in other states. State intervention to assist its portions of the two major metropolitan regions is particularly necessary in light of the need for interstate action in such areas as transportation, port development, water- and air-pollution control, as well as in land-use development.

4. Unitary state control of land use is not feasible. On the land-use control continuum, the opposite of complete home rule is a sweeping transfer of all land-use regulatory powers to the state government. As mentioned earlier, the only comparable example that comes close to this extreme model is the state of Hawaii. But even Hawaii leaves considerable latitude for the counties and larger municipalities. Considering the entrenched attachment to home rule, the fear that intervention by higher levels of government would force sweeping changes in community patterns, and the deep resistance to far-reaching legislative revisions, it is most unlikely that a complete system of state land-use control could be adopted, even if such a measure were deemed desirable.

5. A leadership role must be assumed by the State. On the basis of the rejection of the previous alternatives, it would seem logical for New Jersey to build on recent precedents by further expanding its leadership role in the protection and development of critical areas. The adoption of measures protecting open space, flood plains, coastal wetlands, Hackensack Meadows, Pinelands region, and coastal area facilities indicates that there is wide public and legislative support for a selective state intervention policy, particularly if it is related to the environmental protection and development of critical areas. These measures have been enacted since the early 1960s, in response to an emerging public sensitivity to specific land-use problems. In no sense, however, can this assortment of legislation be considered the equivalent of a comprehensive state land-use policy. What appears to be required is an expansion of the protection and management of critical land resources to include other vulnerable areas subject to new threats and blighted areas requiring redevelopment.

In addition, the state must play an active role in the control of development that has an impact that extends beyond municipal boundaries. This would not only include direct state regulation of major public and private developments in designated critical areas, but also the establishment of state standards and the supervision of local land-use decision-making in certain categories of land-use development. It must be recognized that the intervention of state government in municipal affairs is necessary to insure that responsible local action is taken in respect to transportation, housing, solid waste disposal, and other controversial issues. This implies an acceptance of the notion that the shaping of state land-use policy is a logical arena for the resolution of divergent views that concern crucial land-use issues relating to social and economic problems.

Provisions of the Proposed Community Planning Law (New Jersey Assembly, No. 1422), which deals with the state's implementing and regulating role, are well-intentioned and go in the right direction, but lack the necessary teeth. Although this piece of proposed legislation contains the basic ingredients of a state land-use planning and management system—that is, preparation and adoption of a state development plan; preparation of a capital improvements program; establishment of an official state map; certification of municipal development regulations and developments of regional importance; and the designation and review of municipal regulations governing the development of critical areas—its weakness lies in the fact that municipalities have the option of submitting their regulations and plans to the state for review if they so choose, except in the case of designated critical areas.

In the broader sense, the development of an effective state land-use policy must be grounded in a vision of what the state can realistically achieve within a given period of time. It requires a clear comprehensive picture of New Jersey 10 to 20 years from now in terms of a desirable allocation of its land uses, the nature and distribution of housing, the development and redevelopment of its open and resort areas, and the integration of transportation and other facilities within this developmental framework.

Guidelines for Implementation

The basic prerequisite for effective state land-use policy is a state land-use development plan embracing the visionary as well as the practical.

Create a State Land-Use Resources Commission

As a first step in proceeding with an expanded and improved program of state land-use regulation, New Jersey should establish a state land-use resources commission representing appropriate state staff and line agencies but also drawing extensively for expertise on nationally recognized authorities in the fields of land use, environmental protection, and urban and economic development. The commission would be charged with the primary mission of preparing a preliminary state-wide land-use plan, building on the work of state operating agencies under existing legislation, and making full use of the findings of the current state task force that is examining the state's growth and related problems. In addition to its primary mission, the commission should recommend appropriate legislation, administrative actions, staffing, and funding requirements to permit New Jersey to take advantage of opportunities inherent in existing and prospective federal land-use legislation. It might be remembered that the implementation of well-intentioned and progressive legislation can be hampered by the failure to provide for adequate staffing, as has been the case in Maine and Hawaii.

*Establish a State Mechanism for Land-Use
Leadership, Planning, and Coordination*

In its consideration of preparations required for the advent of a state leadership role under federal legislation, the proposed commission should examine various alternatives for state implementing mechanisms. These include the possibility of establishing a land-use agency as a staff arm of the governor's office, an interagency arrangement representing key planning and operating officials, and a mixed high-level commission of agency officials and citizens of the state. Based on experience in New Jersey and elsewhere, which has amply demonstrated the ineffectiveness of interagency planning, it would be logical to give particular attention to two specific alternatives:

1. Centralizing the land-use coordinating and policy-formulation function within the Governor's office.
2. Creating a new prestigious group outside and above the traditional governmental structure, which would serve as a kind of highest-level planning and adjudicating body to establish policy and settle disputes that cannot be resolved at lower levels.

Create Appropriate Regional Planning Mechanisms

In addition to this attention to an appropriate statewide mechanism, the commission should consider alternative methods for placing municipal land-use regulation into an appropriate regional context. Although it should examine the probability of using county government directly, the commission might well look into the possibility of regionalizing state government by dividing the state into multi-county districts, somewhat on the order of the Vermont system. The counties and municipal government, depending on their capability, might be expected to play a technical assistance, advisory, and review role within such a district framework.

Examine and Adopt Proven Techniques

The commission's examination of appropriate land-use control legislation should include new enabling acts and legislative amendments to strengthen existing tools and to add techniques that have proven effective elsewhere.

    1. *The relative success of New Jersey's Green Acres and acqui-*

sition legislation suggests the desirability of further expanding the use of eminent domain powers and advance land acquisition policies. Not only is it important to set aside needed open space for recreation and conservation purposes by making full use of police power regulations (zoning and subdivision control), compensable regulations, public acquisition of the fee, and public acquisition of less than fee (conservation easements), but it is just as necessary to initiate land banking as a developmental tool. The legislature should authorize the state government, regional development authorities, and municipalities to establish land banks or public land authorities with power to acquire and hold land needed for future development—as sites for various public facilities and as tracts for comprehensively planned private development. Modest state appropriations should be provided as seed money to get land banks started until they can become self-supporting through land sales. Such land banks should take full advantage of acquiring at low or no cost land and/or facilities declared surplus by state and federal agencies. Implementation of this recommendation, while not generating immediate visible results, is an important long-range approach to carrying out state land-use policies and plans.

2. *Both the legislature and appropriate state agencies should take further steps to explore the feasibility of the transferability of development rights for controlling the use and development of land.* Such steps should not only include studies and analyses to refine conceptualization of this approach but should include the drafting of model legislation (guidelines for which are contained in the Appendix to this report) and the authorization of limited demonstrations to test the validity of this approach in the field.

Tax Policy Recommendations

Recognizing that taxation has been neglected as a positive instrument for guiding sound, orderly development, we make the following recommendations in the important area of tax policies:

1. In support of the finding of the Musto Commission that the *excessive reliance on local property taxation to support county and municipal services must be reduced, the state should begin to take over from county and municipal government the fiscal responsibility for such functions and services as education, the administration of*

justice, and welfare—functions financed from property taxes and with state-wide scope, impact, and implications.

2. The Tax Policy Committee's proposal of 1970 for *an experimental limited program of site value taxation for cities over 100,000 population should be implemented.*

Adopt a Mandatory "Fair Share" Regional Housing Policy

New Jersey should adopt a mandatory, controlled system of allocating housing for low- and moderate-income families to suburban and outlying communities. This is one of the principal priorities in regional land-use development. The objective is to devise a policy that removes the land-use barriers restricting low- and moderate-income families to housing choices within the older central cities, while at the same time it provides assurance to suburban communities that they will not be deluged by an influx of low-income migrants.

The Massachusetts experience provides some useful guidelines for designing and carrying out "fair share" housing policies. The fair share approach can take a number of forms, but any successful program must involve housing subsidies, as well as changes in land-use control practices. The Massachusetts experience is instructive. That state's "antisnob" zoning legislation of 1969, establishing a minimum housing quota system for low-income families, has had more psychological than real impact. In practice, large-scale federal and state subsidies have not been available to enable the construction of a significant volume of housing for low-income families. Massachusetts has had somewhat more success in stimulating class mixing through operations of the Massachusetts Housing Finance Agency (MHFA). The MHFA participated in mortgage financing for the construction of some 20,000 housing units during the 1968-1972 period, one-third of which are occupied by low-income families. Most of the units, however, were built in older, urban centers. Of the 6000 units constructed in suburban communities, most of the low- and moderate-income occupants lived in the immediate area of the project site. Consequently, to date, MHFA has had little impact in dispersing low-income residents from central cities to the suburbs.

Strengthen Municipal and County Land-Use Planning

Although the central thrust of the state land-use resources commission would be devoted to land-use regulatory concerns at the state level, the fact that the counties and to a greater extent the municipalities would continue to have major land-use responsibilities suggests that the commission should devote a significant portion of its time to devising ways for strengthening the municipal and county planning function. What appears to be needed is a stronger version of those provisions in the "Proposed Community Planning Law" (New Jersey Assembly, No. 1422) pertaining to municipal and regional planning and land-use control. As mentioned earlier, there are basic weaknesses in state enabling legislation dealing with local land-use regulation; moreover, in many instances, counties and municipalities lack the will, capacity, and funding to carry out the intent of enabling legislation.

The commission might consider legislation to make existing enabling acts in land-use control mandatory rather than permissive and to incorporate innovative alternatives tested in other states (and discussed in this report) into the state's enabling acts. These include incentive zoning, environmental impact controls, land banking, and most especially, use of transfer of development rights. Consideration should be given to methods of making available requisite technical assistance and funding to help counties and municipalities adopt and implement these relatively sophisticated land-use control systems.

As is noted in Chapter 2, incentive zoning establishes arrangements whereby developers can be granted permission to develop properties more intensively in return for including certain desirable features such as additional open space or parking area in their plans. Although this technique has been mainly used in densely settled urban areas in connection with high-rise office buildings, there would appear to be no reason why it could not be adopted for use in suburban areas, including the areas outside PUDs and new communities.

Under the heading of environmental controls, this report recommends that the state expand its presently limited review and approval function, which is now restricted to selected environmentally sensitive areas, to include all major and private developments throughout the state. The experience in California, Massachusetts, and Vermont can provide valuable guidelines. There are two major issues in implementing a comprehensive approach to environmental control: (1) the pressing need for reconciling environmental protection with economic development, including employment generation and energy production and distribution; (2) the absolute necessity of creating an experienced, substantial, and highly professional staff to implement environmental control procedures expeditiously and soundly.

Appendix: Draft of Development Rights Legislation with Commentary

The following is a detailed draft of proposed development rights legislation for the state of New Jersey. Each section of the draft is followed by a short commentary intended to explain the terminology of that section and to clarify what it authorizes and prescribes.

1. Grant of Power to Local Government

The power of zoning granted by the provisions in (State Enabling Legislation) shall include the power to provide for open space preservation districts wherein the use of land may be restricted to agriculture, conservation or recreation or any combination thereof and only such buildings or structures which are incidental to the permitted land uses and approved by the planning Board shall be constructed.

Any municipality may by ordinance amend its zoning regulations to provide for an open space preservation district, subject to the provisions of this act. The enactment of an ordinance or amendment thereto pursuant to the powers granted herein shall be in accordance with the procedure required for the adoption of an amendment to the zoning ordinance as provided in (applicable provision of State Enabling Legislation.)

Commentary. This legislation does not disturb the existing allocation of the power of land-use regulation to local governments. Some members of the committee urged that regulating authority be vested in a state agency, rather than in local governments. However, the limited political feasibility of approval of such a proposal was the primary reason for retaining local control. The last paragraph seeks to retain the existing procedure in most states by which the Planning Board participates in the process for amending the zoning ordinance.

2. Creation of Open Space Preservation Districts

(a) The governing body may create open space preservation districts of such numbers, shapes and areas as it may deem necessary to carry out the purposes of this act, provided that (i) all land in each district is substantially undeveloped farmland, woodland, flood plain, swamp, marsh, or land of steep slope, and that farmland or woodland, or a combination thereof shall constitute more than sixty percent of all the land in the open space preservation district; and, (ii) the location of each district is consistent with and corresponds to the master plan of the municipality; and, (iii) the aggregate size of the districts bear a reasonable relationship to the present and future patterns of population growth set forth in the zoning ordinance and master plan; and, (iv) the land in each district is not less than twenty-five contiguous acres.

Commentary. Subsection (a) makes it clear that the open space preservation plan must be based upon the municipal master plan with particular reference to studies of future population projections and topographical, soil, and other land-use studies. In the process of computing the amount of land required to meet various municipal needs and designation of land most appropriate to meet those needs, land will be designated for open space preservation. To avoid the designation of open space districts too small to be effective, a minimum size of 25 contiguous acres is prescribed. The land in any open space preservation district may be comprised of any combination of the enumerated types of undeveloped land but must contain at least 60 percent farmland, woodland, or a combination thereof. The purpose of this provision is to preserve land that might otherwise be developed in addition to swamp, marsh, flood plain, and other land of limited utility for development.

(b) Land zoned exclusively for commercial, industrial or other non-residential use at the time of the adoption of an ordinance pursuant to this act shall not be included in an open space preservation district.

Commentary. Subsection (b) is intended to exclude land zoned for commercial or industrial uses from open space preservation districts. There are two reasons for this exclusion. The primary reason is based upon the committee's determination to limit the application of the program to *residential* development. The committee concluded that if development rights are issued for commercial and industrial development, the program would become too complex to administer. The second reason for the exclusion of commercial and industrial property is that land zoned for those purposes may be too expensive or otherwise inappropriate for open space preservation. The committee was not unmindful of the fact that some municipalities zone unrealistically large proportions of undeveloped land for commercial and industrial uses as an extralegal technique of retarding residential development.[1] In such jurisdictions a realistic rezoning of such areas will be required before adopting an ordinance pursuant to the provisions of this act.

(c) Any nonconforming use or structure existing in the open space preservation district at the time of adoption thereof may be continued and in the event of partial destruction of such non-conforming use or structure it may be restored or repaired.

Commentary. Subsection (c) is intended to protect the right of farmers, particularly, and others who have existing structures that do not conform to the restricted use on open space preservation land.

(d) Subject to subsections (e) and (f) of this section, all proposals for the construction or enlargement of a building, or other structure in an open space preservation district, shall be made to the planning board for review and recommendation after a public hearing and shall be submitted to the governing body for approval after favorable referral by the planning board.

Commentary. Subsection (d) is intended to require all proposals for construction in open space preservation districts to be subjected to the scrutiny of the planning board and the governing body. It is contemplated that farm residences, agricultural buildings, stables, and other structures not inconsistent with open space preservation will be permitted, but only with the approval of both governmental bodies.

(e) Land within the open space preservation district may be subdivided pursuant to (Subdivision Enabling Legislation) only for the purpose of transferrring ownership of the sub-divided parcel for farming purposes and a residential dwelling may be constructed on the subdivided parcel only if such parcel contains at least twenty-five acres.

Commentary. Subsection (e) is intended to restrict the subdivision of land in open space preservation districts. The only exception permitted is subdivision of farmland into a parcel of not less than 25 acres. This exception was made to permit farmers who wish to do so to subdivide their land among their children.

(f) A variance for a use of land not otherwise permitted in an open space preservation district may be granted by the governing body after favorable referral by the local planning board and by the appropriate state agency only for a development proposal which is reasonably necessary to protect public health or safety and no practical alternative to the proposed development is available. Otherwise no variance for a change of use or zoning amendment shall be approved to permit development in an open space preservation district other than for uses which conform to the provisions of section 1 of this act.

Commentary. Subsection (f) transfers the power to grant a variance in an open space preservation district from the zoning board to the governing body, which in turn must obtain the approval from both the planning board and the appropriate state agency. This provision is intended to protect the integrity of the program from the kind of influences often exerted upon zoning boards.

3. Certificates of Development Rights

(a) The ordinance creating an open space preservation district shall also provide for the establishment and distribution of certificates of development rights by the owners of land in the open space preservation district and shall further provide that an increase in the density of the development hereinafter provided for in section (b) shall not be permitted unless the applicant therefor submits for cancellation the required number of certificates of development rights.

Commentary. This subsection authorizes the creation of an innovative legal instrument, that is, the certificate of development rights. Certificates will be inscribed in specific denominations and will be transferable by endorsement and registration as provided in subsection (b). Certificates will be issued to owners of land designated for open space. Owners of developable land will have to purchase these certificates to increase the density of development of their land. Thus, both a supply of and demand for certificates is created.

(b) Certificates of development rights, issued by the municipality pursuant to the provisions of this act, shall be recorded in the office of the County Clerk of the county in which the municipality is located. The sale and transfer of certificates of development rights shall be regulated and recorded in the same manner as the sale and transfer of real property. Upon exercise of a certificate of development right pursuant to Section 6 (b) herein and upon the issuance of a building permit therefor, the certificate of development right shall be cancelled by the municipal official designated for that purpose. Notice of cancellation shall be given by said municipal official to the County Clerk, who shall record the cancellation of the certificate.

Commentary. This subsection authorizes the creation of a recording system for certificates of development rights similar to the recording system for other instruments of real estate conveyance. When the owner of land designated for open space sells his certificates to an owner of developable land (or to anyone else, such as a broker or speculator), the transfer will be recorded by the County Clerk. When the development rights are used to obtain a building permit, the certificates are cancelled. When all the authorized certificates are cancelled, the remaining owners of developable land will be limited to the restricted use designated in the zoning ordinance, that is, single family residences. These constraints will tend to keep the certificates marketable as long as there is demand for residential development at increased densities. The market value of development rights will respond to the same economic forces as the market value of developable residential land. If an owner of development rights holds out for too high a price, the owners of developable land will tend to buy the rights from someone else or will use their land for single family residences.

4. Establishment of Development Rights

(a) The planning board, after public hearing with personal notice to all owners of land in the proposed open space preservation districts, shall recommend to the governing body for adoption the total number of units of development rights for distribution to all owners of property in the proposed open space preservation districts.

Commentary. This provision designates the planning board as the appropriate agency to establish the plan for the computation of the number and the allocation of the development rights. A public hearing is required to permit interested persons, and particularly owners of land in the open space preservation districts, to examine the objectives of the plan and the method of computation of the number of development rights to be distributed. After such hearing, the planning board makes its recommendation to the governing body for adoption.

(b) The total number of development rights for which certificates shall be issued shall be equal to and deemed to represent the full and total residential development potential of all undeveloped real property in the jurisdiction in excess of the restricted development authorized for developable residential land pursuant to the zoning regulations controlling development therein.

Commentary. This provision sets forth the basic principle that the quantum of residential development shall be prescribed by the number of development rights authorized and distributed plus a limited amount possible under restrictive zoning regulations. For example, if the plan calls for a limit of 1000 residential units and if developable land under the zoning ordinance is limited to 200 units (for example, 200 acres restricted to one residential unit per acre), then certificates equal to no more than 800 development rights may be issued. Thus, the total number of development rights issued will be equal to the total development potential less the number of units permissible without use of development rights.

5. Distribution of Residential Development Rights

(a) The total number of certificates of development rights determined pursuant to section 4 herein shall be distributed in accordance with subsection (b) of this section to all owners of land in the open space preservation district. For purposes of distribution of certificates of development rights, ownership of land shall be determined as of the date of the adoption of the ordinance creating the open space preservation district.

Commentary. This provision calls for the distribution of the development rights to the owners of open space land. The certificates of development rights that they receive provide the compensation for their loss of the right to develop their land. The right to receive development rights vests at the time of adoption of the local ordinance. As a result, when enactment of a development rights ordinance is anticipated, the market value of open space land will reflect the value of the development rights attached to it.

(b) To provide a just and equitable distribution of certificates of development rights the number of such certificates distributed to an individual property owner shall be equal to a percentage calculated by comparing the market value of the individual's property to the market value of all property in the open space preservation district on the date of adoption of the open space preservation district.

Commentary. This subsection provides the method of allocation of the previously determined total of development rights in the jurisdiction to the owners of open space land. Each owner is entitled to the same proportion of the total number of development rights as the value of his open space land bears to the total value of all land designated for open space preservation. This method of allocation is based upon the recognition that acreage alone is an insufficient basis of allocation of development rights because some land has greater value than other land because of its development potential prior to the adoption of the development rights ordinance. Under this provision the owner of the more valuable land will receive a greater proportion of the total number of development rights.

(c) To implement this section the planning board shall review the assessed value of all property in the open space preservation district in order to establish market value on an equalized basis for the purpose of ensuring just distribution of certificates of development rights. The planning board shall hold special hearings with personal notice to all owners of property in the proposed open space preservation district to review all appraisals and consider such objections as may be presented, and shall take such action as it deems necessary to ensure the just distribution of development rights.

Commentary. This subsection is intended to provide an open procedure to assure a fair distribution of development rights among owners of open space land. Notice of all appraisals of land in the open space preservation districts will be given to all owners of open space land. Open hearings on the issue of value will allow each owner to compare the assessed value of his property with the assessed value of all other open space land.

(d) Any owner of property in the open space preservation district may appeal any determination made under this section to the (appropriate court).

Commentary. This subsection provides a judicial remedy for owners of open space land who feel aggrieved by the allocation of development rights.

6. Marketability of Residential Development Rights

(a) To create an incentive for the purchase of development rights, the governing body, by amendment to the zoning ordinance, shall designate specific zoning districts wherein the permissable residential dwelling unit density may be increased to a specified range of densities. Such zoning districts shall be designated for use and densities consistent with the master plan to create a greater incentive to develop land in such districts with certificates of development rights than without such certificates.

Commentary. This subsection provides for the designation of zoning districts in which higher densities will be permitted if the owner acquires development rights. Increased density is to be authorized only where such density would be appropriate as determined by the land-use plan and where there would be market demand for development at higher densities. The existence of this economic incentive is critically important because, unless there is a market for housing at higher densities in the district so designated therefor, there will be no market for the development rights and no compensation for the owners of land preserved for open space. On the other hand, if there is no market for housing at higher densities anywhere in the jurisdiction, then the claim of compensation by owners of open space land is probably equally remote and premature.

(b) Developmemt of prescribed higher densities shall be permitted as a matter of right if the applicant proposing such higher density owns development rights certificates in an amount equal in number to the increase in dwelling unit density above the number of dwelling units permitted under the zoning regulations.

Commentary. This is the provision that authorizes higher densitites in designated districts to the extent permitted by the zoning ordinance if the owner has a sufficient number of development rights for such increased density. This provision presupposes the existence of height and bulk regulations in other sections of the zoning ordinance to the extent that such regulations are necessary to prevent over-crowding of the area and overutilization of neighborhood facilities.

(c) Development proposals consistent with the residential density requirements of the zoning regulations may be approved at such lower density without the requirement of certificates of development rights. However, if the development proposals are approved at the lower density and as a result thereof an imbalance is created whereby the number of uncancelled certificates of development rights exceeds the amount of undeveloped land upon which certificates of development rights may be exercised, the governing body may amend the zoning ordinance to rectify the imbalance to maintain the marketability of the outstanding development rights certificates.

Commentary. The first sentence of this subsection authorizes the development of land in developable districts at the lower authorized density. For example, an owner of an acre of land on which one residential unit per acre is permitted may build that one unit without the use of development rights. This provision is designed to overcome objection to the plan by owners of developable land who are content with that restricted use. An owner of developable land has a number of choices:(1) he can build in accordance with the lower authorized density; (2) he can purchase development rights and build at a higher density; or (3) he can sell his land to others for development at higher densities.

The last sentence of this paragraph is intended to deal with the unlikely possibility that most owners of developable land will act against their economic self-interest and develop their land at the lower density in spite of market demand for more intensive use of their land. In such event, owners of open space land would not be compensated because the demand for their development rights requires the existence of land developable at higher densities. Under these circumstances, the governing body is authorized to designate additional districts of developable land for which the development rights may be used to meet a projected housing need and the market demand based thereon.

(d) No variance for residential use at increased densities

shall be granted pursuant to (appropriate section of state enabling legislation) unless the applicant provides evidence of ownership of certificates of development rights in an amount sufficient to authorize a higher density under the provisions of this act. No building permit shall be issued upon such variances unless the requisite number of certificates of development rights are attached to said application for cancellation.

Commentary. This provision is designed to protect the integrity of the plan from derogation by the variance procedure. Without this provision, the entire plan could be frustrated by use variances for residential development. Under this provision a use variance for residential units can be issued only if the applicant owns a sufficient number of development rights and is prepared to surrender them for cancellation when application is made for a building permit.

7. Taxation

(a) Certificates of development rights shall be taxed in the same manner as real property is taxed. The assessed value of each uncancelled certificate, in the year of adoption of a development rights ordinance, shall be equal to the difference between the aggregate value of all undeveloped land zoned for restricted residential use and the aggregate value of said land if developed with the use of all development rights issued, divided by the total number of development rights issued. Thereafter, current sales of certificates of development rights in that jurisdiction shall constitute evidence of market value for tax-assessment purposes.

Commentary. This subsection provides the basic guidelines for the taxation of development rights. Because they represent a substantial part of the value of undeveloped land, development rights are to be taxed as real property. When the ordinance is first enacted, the aggregate value of all outstanding development rights will be the difference between the value of all residential land if fully developed with development rights and the value of the same land for restricted residential development, as illustrated by the following example:

	Aggregate value of the land only
200 acres developed with 1000 residential units (with development rights)	$5,000,000
200 acres developed with 200 residential units (restricted use)	1,000,000
Value of 800 development rights	$4,000,000
Value of 1 development right	$ 5,000

The underlying assumption of this calculation is that an owner would be willing to pay for a development right an amount of money equal to the increment in value of the land resulting from the use of that development right—in the above illustration, $5000. As soon as a market for development rights is established in the jurisdiction, actual sales will provide evidence of value for assessment purposes.

(b) Land in the open space preservation district shall be assessed at its value for agricultural or other open space use.

Commentary. This subsection gives effect to the fact that once the development right is removed from the land in open space preservation districts, the value of that land is limited to its agricultural or other open space use.

(c) Tax exemption—DELETED

Commentary. The original draft of the proposed New Jersey legislation contains a provision exempting development rights from taxation if issued to and held by an owner of land qualified for tax exemption under the New Jersey Farmland Assessment Act. This provision is not recommended because such tax exemption: (1) would tend to discourage the marketability of development rights while held by farmers; (2) would impose an unnecessary additional tax burden on other taxpayers; and (3) give an unjustified advantage to owners of farmland who may thereby continue to use the land for farm purposes and reap the advantages of increasing value of development rights without corresponding tax liability.

8. Effective Date

This act shall become effective 12 months after enactment therof and during the said 12 month period the (appropirate state agency) shall conduct such studies as may be necessary to prepare model ordinances, suggested rules and regulations and other studies that will assist municipalities in the adoption and implementation of the powers granted herein. An appropriation of ($_____) is authorized for this purpose.

Commentary. This last provision conveys the unanimous opinion of the members of the drafting committee that there are still undiscovered implications and effects of this proposal that require additional investigation and study.

Notes

Chapter 1
Introduction

1. For an in-depth discussion of PUB's advantages, see Robert W. Burchell, *Planned Unit Development: New Communities American Style* (New Brunswick, N.J.: Center for Urban Policy Research, Rutgers University, 1972), pp. 6-30.

2. Office of Business Economics, Division of Planning and Research, New Jersey Department of Labor and Industry, *State of New Jersey Residential Construction Authority for Building Permits Annual, Summary 1972* (Trenton, N.J.: October 1973).

3. "New Jersey Municipal Planned Unit Development Act," in *Laws of New Jersey, 1967*, c. 61, Sec. 1(d).

4. R. W. Burchell, op. cit., pp. 65-77.

5. Richard H. Slavin, "Toward a State Land Use Policy: Harmonizing Development and Conservation," *State Government: The Journal of State Affairs*, XLIV, No. 1 (Lexington, Ky.: Council of State Governments, Winter 1971), pp. 2-11.

6. Ibid.

Chapter 2
Control of Land Development by Application of Police Power

1. N. J. Stat. Ann., Sec. 40:55-30 et seq.

2. N. J. Stat. Ann., Sec. 40:55-1.14 et seq.

3. N. J. Acts (1953), c. 434.

4. N. J. Acts (1967), c. 61.

5. Robert W. Burchell, *Planned Unit Development: New Communities American Style* (New Brunswick, N. J.: Center for Urban Policy Research, Rutgers University, 1972), p. 6.

6. N. J. Stat. Ann., Sec. 40:27-1 et seq.

7. State of New Jersey County and Municipal Government Study Commission, Second Report, *County Government: Challenge and Change* (Trenton, N. J., 28 April 1969).

8. N. J. Stat. Ann., Secs. 13:17-1 et seq., 13:1 B-13 et seq. [N. J. Acts (1961), c. 404].

9. N. J. Stat. Ann., Sec. 13:19A-1 et seq.

10. N. J. Acts (1972), c. 185.

11. Rose, *From the Legislatures: Use of Flood Prone Land,*[1] REAL ESTATE L.J. 382 (Spring 1973).

12. Morris County Land Improvement Co. v. Parsippany-Troy Hills Township, 40 N.J. 539, 193 A.2d 232 (1963).

13. For a perceptive analysis of controls for natural processes, see Ann Louise Strong, "Incentives and Controls for Open Space," in *Metropolitan Open Space and Natural Process*, ed. David A. Wallace (Philadelphia: University of Pennsylvania Press, 1970).

14. Morris County Land Improvement Co. v. Parsippany-Troy Hills Township, op. cit., note 13.

15. Lake Intervale Homes, Inc. v. Parsippany-Troy Hills Township, 28 N.J. 423, 147 A.2d 28 (1958).

16. Lomarch Corp. v. Mayor of Englewood, 51 N.J. 108, 237 A.2d 881 (1968).

17. The new issues being faced by the courts are discussed in Jerome G. Rose, "The Courts and the Balanced Community: Recent Trends in New Jersey Zoning Law," *Journal of the American Institute of Planners*, 39 (July 1973), p. 265.

18. Golden v. Planning Board of Town of Ramapo, 30 N.Y. 2d 359, 285 N.E. 2d 291 (1972). Appeal to the U. S. Supreme Court dismissed for want of a substantial federal question, 409 U.S. 1003 (1972).

19. O'Keefe, *Time Controls on Land Use: Prophylatic Law for Planners*, 57 CORNELL L. REV. 846 (1972). © Copyright 1972 by Cornell University.

20. Ibid., pp. 848-849.

21. See Earl Finkler, *Nongrowth as a Planning Alternative: A Preliminary Examination of an Emerging Issue* (Chicago: American Society of Planning Officials, September 1972), Rept. No. 283.

22. Golden v. Planning Board of Town of Ramapo, op. cit.

23. 285 N.E. 2d 302.

24. H. Franklin, *Controlling Urban Growth–But For Whom?* (Washington, D.C.: The Potomac Institute, Inc., 1973); see also: Note, *Time Controls on Land Use: Prophylatic Law for Planners*, 57 CORNELL L. REV. 827 (1972); E. Finkler, op. cit.; Comment, *Golden v. Town of Ramapo: Establishing a New Dimension in American Planning Law*, 4 THE URBAN LAWYER ix (1972).

25. H. Franklin, op. cit., p. 20.

26. Ibid., pp. 31-36.

27. Rodgers v. Village of Tarrytown, 302 N.Y. 115, 06 N.E.2d 731 (1951).

28. Huff v. Board of Zoning Appeals, 214 Md. 48, 133 A.2d 83 (1959).

29. Rockwell v. Township of Chesterfield Township, 23 N.J. 117, 128 A.2d 473 (1957).

30. APSO Zoning Digest (Chicago: *American Society of Planning Officials*, 1970), 22 ZD1 Connecticut, p. 30.

31. Platt, *Valid Spot Zoning: A Creative Tool for Flexibility of Land Use*, 48 OREGON L. REV. 251 (1969). Reprinted by permission. Copyright © 1969 by University of Oregon. Small area zoning has been upheld in such states as Connecticut, Maryland, Oregon, and Wisconsin.

32. Trager, *Contract Zoning*, 23 MARYLAND L. REV. 122 (1963). See also Shapiro, *The Case for Conditional Zoning*, 41 TEMPLE LAW Q. 267 (1968).

33. San Francisco Amended Ord. 274-68; approved 16 Sept. 1968.

34. Benson, *Bonus or Incentive Zoning: Legal Implications*, 21 SYRACUSE L. REV. 905 (1970).

35. Article XI, Proposed Zoning Ordinance, Rome, N.Y.: cited in Robert M. Anderson, *American Law of Zoning* (Rochester, N.Y.: Lawyers Co-operative, 1968), Sec. 26.58.

36. Hirsch, *Measuring the Good Neighbor: A New Look at Performance Standards in Zoning*, 2 LAND USE CONTROLS 15 (Spring 1968). See also Gillespie, *Industrial Zoning and Beyond: Compatibility through Performance Standards*, 46 J. URBAN L. 723 (1969).

37. For a thorough discussion of open space zoning, see Kusler,

Open Space Zoning: Valid Regulations or Invalid Taking, 57 MINN. L. REV. 1 (1972).

38. City of Plainfield v. Borough of Middlesex, 69 N.J. Supra 136, 173 A.2d 785 (Law Div., 1961), in *Techniques for Preserving Open Spaces*, 75 HARVARD L. REV. 1624-1625 (1962).

39. Fisher v. Bedminster Township, 11 N.J. 194, 93 A.2d 378 (1952).

40. Board of County Supervisors of Fairfax County v. Carper, 200 Va. 653, 107 S.E.2d 390 (1959).

41. Township and Freeholders v. Schire, 119 N.J. Supra 433, A.2d (cert. denied), 41 U.S.L.W. 3445 (1973), where the U.S. Supreme Court refused to review a N.Y. Supreme Court decision invalidating a 40,000 square foot minimum lot size for residential development.

42. Ayres v. City Council, 34 Cal. 2d 31, 207 P.2d 1 (1949).

43. Miller v. City of Beaver Falls, 368 Pa. 198, 82 A.2d 34 (1951).

44. Kelber v. City of Upland, 155 Cal. App. 2d 631, 318 P.2d 561 (Dist. Ct. App.) (1957).

45. *Techniques for Preserving Open Spaces*, 75 HARVARD L. REV. 1629 (1962).

46. 42 U.S.C., Sec. 4331 et seq. (1970).

47. James A. Roberts, "Just What Is An Environmental Impact Statement?" *Urban Land* (May 1973), p. 11.

48. Calif. Pub. Resources Code, Secs. 2100-21151.

49. Roberts, op. cit., p. 12.

Chapter 3
Control of Land Development Through Use of Eminent Domain

1. See Rindge Co. v. County of Los Angeles, 262 U.S. 702 (1923).

2. See City and County of Honolulu v. Bishop Trust Company, 49 Hawaii 494, 421 P.2d 300 (1966).

3. Berman v. Parker, 348 U.S. 26 (1954).

4. *Problems of Advance Land Acquisition,* 52 Minn. L. Rev. 1176 (1968). For a detailed review of foreign practices in land banking, see K.L. Parsons et al., *Public Land Acquisition for New*

Communities and the Control of Urban Growth: Alternative Strategies (Ithaca, N.Y.: Center for Urban Development Research, Cornell University, March 1973).

5. N. J. Stat. Ann., Sec. 20.

6. N. J. Stat. Ann., Sec. 40:61-1 et seq. Several cases upheld the validity of eminent domain power for these purposes. Guild v. City of Newark, 87 N.J. Eq. 38, 99 A. 120 (1916), and Soper v. Conly, 108 N.J. Eq. 370, 154 A. 852 (1931), affirmed 107 N.J. Eq. 537, 153 A. 586.

7. N. J. Stat. Ann., Sec. 13:8A-6 (1961).

8. N. J. Acts (1971) c. 419.

9. N. J. Stat. Ann., Sec. 58:16A-1 et seq.

10. N. J. Stat. Ann., Sec. 55:14E. The courts have held the public purpose of this chapter valid—providing adequate public housing by enlisting the participation of private capital. See Redfern v. Board of Commissioners of Jersey City, 137 N.J.L. 356, 59 A.2d 641 (1948).

11. National Commission on Urban Problems, *Building the American City* (Washington, D.C.: United States Government Printing Office, 1968), p. 251.

12. See Hans Calinfors, Francine F. Rabinowitz, and Daniel J. Oresch, *Urban Government for Greater Stockholm* (New York: Frederick Praeger, Inc., 1967), pp. 99-102.

13. Marion Clawson, *Suburban Land Conversion in the United States,* Resources for the Future (Baltimore, Md.: Johns Hopkins Press, 1971), p. 356.

14. Canadian Federal Task Force on Housing and Urban Development, *Report* (Ottawa: Queen's Printer, 1969), p. 43.

15. Robert, *The Demise of Property Law,* 57 CORNELL L. REV. 44 (1971). © Copyright 1971 by Cornell University.

16. Ibid., p. 46. Commonwealth of Puerto Rico v. Rosso, 95 P.R.Rep. 488 (1967), upheld the validity of early land acquisition.

17. For a further discussion of land banking as a device to order urban growth and of the organizational, legal, and financial condemnations of land banking, see Fishman and Gross, *Public Land Banking: A New Praxis for Urban Growth,* 23 CASE WEST. RES. L. REV. 896 (Summer 1972).

18. Carlor Co. v. Miami, 62 So.2d 897 (Fla.); cert. denied, 346 U.S. 821 (1953).

19. State v. Chang, 46 Hawaii 279, 378 P.2d 882 (1963).

20. Board of Education v. Baczewski, 340 Mich. 265, 65 N.W.2d 810 (1954).

21. Port of Everett v. Everett Improvement Company, 124 Wash. 486, 214 P. 1064 (1923).

22. State Road Department v. Southerland, Inc., 117 So.2d, 512 Fla. (1960). For a useful and extensive discussion of the constitutional issues surrounding advance land acquisition, see Note, *Problems of Advance Land Acquisition,* 52 MINN. L. REV. 1175 (1968).

23. For a detailed discussion of the legal theories of excess condemnation, see Note *Excess Condemnation—To Take or Not to Take—a Functional Analysis.* 15 N.Y.L.REV. (1969).

24. For a further discussion of the historical basis, theory applications, issues, and proposals for constitutional and statutory changes relating to excess condemnation see Matheson, *Excess Condemnation in California: Proposals for Statutory and Constitutional Change,* 42 SO. CAL. L. REV. 421 (1969).

25. William H. Whyte, *Open Space Action* Report to the Outdoor Recreation Resources Review Commission (Washington, D.C.: Outdoor Recreation Resources Review Commission, 1962), Rept. 15.

26. See *Techniques for Preserving Open Spaces,* 75 HARVARD L. REV. 1622 (1962), and Eveleth, *An Appraisal of Techniques to Preserve Open Space,* 9. VILL. L. REV. 551 (1964), in addition to 52 MINN. L. REV. Note, 1175 (1968).

27. A modified version of the negative conservation easement was proposed by Jan Krasnowiecki and Ann Louise Strong. See "Compensable Regulations for Open Space: A Means of Controlling Urban Growth," *Journal of the American Institute of Planners,* 29 (May 1963), p. 87. For a detailed discussion of the legal, administrative, and valuation problems connected with scenic easements, see Donald F. Sutte, Jr., and Roger A. Cunningham, *Scenic Easements, Legal Administrative and Valuation Problems and Procedures* (Washington, D.C.: Highway Research Board, 1968), National Cooperative High Research Program Rept. 56.

28. Danziger, *Control of Urban Sprawl or Securing Open Space: Regulation by Condemnation or by Ordinance?* 50 CAL. L. REV. 483 (1962).

Chapter 4
Control of Land Development Through Taxation Policies

1. For a penetrating examination of the effects of property taxes on urban development, see Dick Netzer, *Impact of the Property Tax: Its Economic Implications for Urban Problems* (May 1968); prepared for the consideration of the National Commission on Urban Problems (Washington, D.C., Research Report 1).

2. Ibid., p. 6.

3. For a detailed examination of constitutional problems relating to land-use taxation, see Hagman, *Open Space Planning and Property Taxation–Some Suggestions*, 1964 WISC. L. REV. 628-657. (1964).

4. *Summary of the Report of the New Jersey Tax Policy Committee* (Trenton, N.J., Feb. 23, 1972), p. 21; report submitted to Governor William T. Cahill pursuant to Exec. Order No. 5 of 1970.

5. Mason Gaffney, "Land Planning and the Property Tax," *Journal of the American Institute of Planners,* 35 (1969), pp. 181-183. Land value taxation accomplishes Gaffney's items 4-7 because of the ability it gives communities to negotiate the improvements with the developer.

6. *Site Valuation as a Base for Local Taxation,* Canadian Tax Foundation Conference Report (Toronto: Canadian Tax Foundation, 1961), pp. 15-16.

7. *Summary of the Report of the New Jersey Tax Policy Committee,* op. cit., pp. 21-22.

8. *Summary of the Report of the New Jersey Tax Policy Committee,* op. cit., pp. 23-24. The decline in farm acreage has continued since 1969, although at a slower pace. Between 1964 and 1969, losses of farmland totaled 220,000 acres as compared with 45,000 acres between 1969 and 1973.

9. *Summary of the Report of the New Jersey Tax Policy Committee,* op. cit., p. 24.

10. Delogu, *The Taxing Power as a Land Use Control Device,* 45 DENVER L.J. 279 (1968).

11. For a detailed discussion of the Hawaiian system, see Hagman, *The Single Tax and Land-Use Planning: Henry George updated,* 12 U.C.L.A. L. REV. 782-788 (1962).

12. Hawaii Rev. Laws, Secs. 98H, 128-2, -9(d), -9.2, -13, -28, 129-2 (Supp. 1963); Secs. 98H-1, -2 (Supp. 1963); Secs. 98H-5, -6 (Supp. 1963); Secs. 128-2, -8, -9, -14 (Supp. 1963).

13. Hawaii Rev. Laws, Sec. 242-12 (1968).

14. See Holmes, *Assessment of Farmland Under the California Land Conservation Act and the 'Breathing Space' Amendment,* 55 CAL. L. REV. 273 (1967).

15. See "Saving the Land," *Time* (May 28, 1973), p. 96.

16. Rose, *Vermont Uses the Taxing Power to Control Land Use,* 2 REAL ESTATE L. J. 602 (1973).

17. For an extensive discussion of state tax policy in this field, see Farnum Alston, "Preferential Taxation of Agricultural and Open Space Lands: A Proposal for Wisconsin," Working Paper 8F (Dec. 1972), prepared for Faculty Land-Use Problem Definition Seminar. Available from the Institute for Environmental Studies, University of Wisconsin, Madison, Wisc.

Chapter 5
Preservation of Open Space Through Transfer of Development Rights

1. American students of British land use planning have observed and reported on developments in the British experiment in land use planning over the years. The following, in chronological sequence, is a bibliography of those reports: D. POOLEY, THE EVOLUTION OF BRITISH PLANNING LEGISLATION (Legislative Research Center, University of Michigan Law School, 1960); Mandelker, *Notes from the English: Compensation in Town and Country Planning,* 49 CAL. L. REV. 699 (1961); D. HEAP, AN OUTLINE OF PLANNING LAW (4th ed. 1963); D. HEAP, INTRODUCING THE LAND COMMISSION ACT (1972); Heap, *The Taxation of Development Value in Land: The English Bill for a Land Commission,* TRENDS (ASPO 1967); Garner, *Introduction to English Planning Law,* 24 OKLA. L. REV. 457 (1971); Garner & Callies, *Planning Law in England, the Wales and the United States,* 1 ANGLO-AMERICAN L. REV. 434 (1972); Hagman, *Planning Blight, Participation and Just Compensation: Anglo-American Comparisons,* 4 THE URBAN LAWYER 434 (1972); Moore, *Planning in Britain: The Changing Scene,* 1972 URBAN LAW ANNUAL 89.

2. Royal Comm'n on the Distribution of the Industrial Population, Report, Cmd. No. 6153 (1940).

3. Expert Committee on Compensation and Betterment, Final Report, Cmd. No. 6386 (1942).

4. Committee on Land Utilization in Rural Area, Report, Cmd. No. 6378 (1942).

5. *See* D. Pooley, *supra* note 1, at 27.

6. House of Lords Paper 159 at 1894, quoted in Uthwatt Report, para. 259 at 104; *see* D. Pooley, *supra* note 1, at 17.

7. 10 & 11 Geo. 6, c.51.

8. "Indeed, after July 1, 1948, ownership of land carries with it nothing more than the bare right to go on using it for its existing purpose. The owner has no right to develop it, that is to say, he has no right to build on it and no right to change its use." D. Heap, An Outline of Planning Law 12 (1963).

9. Town and Country Planning in Britain (Central Office of Information Reference Pamphlet No. 9, 1962).

10. D. Pooley, *supra* note 1, at 84.

11. 1 & 2 Eliz. 2, c.16; 2 & 3 Eliz. 2, c.72.

12. "I would be the last person to say I understand the Bill," a statement made by the Lord Chancellor on December 6, 1966 during the House of Lords debate on the Land Commission Bill, as cited in D. Heap, Introducing the Land Commission Act (1967).

13. Land Commission Act, 1967, c. 1.

14. Land Commission (Dissolution) Act of 1971; *see* Moore, *supra* note 1, at 91 and 93.

15. Weissburg, *Legal Alternatives to Police Power: Condemnation and Purchase, Development Rights, Gifts* in Open Space and the Law (F. Herring ed. 1965); N. Williams, Land Acquisition for Outdoor Recreation: analysis of Selected Legal Problems (U.S. Outdoor Recreation Resources Review Comm. Study Report No. 16, 1963).

16. W. Whyte, Securing Open Space for Urban America: Conservation Easements (Urban Land Inst. Tech. Bull. No. 36, 1959).

17. Keppell v. Bailey, 2 Myl. & K. 517, 535, 39 Eng. Rep. 1042, 1049 (Ch. 1834).

18. 2 American Law of Property §§ 8.78-8.83 (Casner ed. 1952).

19. *Id*. at §§ 8.73; *see also* Eveleth, *Appraisal of Techniques to Preserve Open Space,* 9 VILL. L. REV. 559 (1964).

20. *See* State *ex. rel.* Twin City Bldg. & Inv. Co. v. Houghton, 144 Minn. 1, 174 N.W. 885 (1919).

21. Sacramento Municipal Util. Dist. v. Pacific Gas & Elec. Co., 72 Cal. App. 2d 638, 165 P.2d 741 (Dist. Ct. App. 1946).

22. *In re* City of New York, 57 App. Div. 166, 68 N.Y.S. 196, *aff'd mem.,* 167 N.Y. 624, 60 N.E. 1108 (1901).

23. N.J. STAT. ANN. § 13:8A-12 (1961) (emphasis added).

24. CAL. GOV'T. CODE § 6950 (emphasis added.)

25. VT. STAT. ANN. tit. 10, § 6303(b) (Supp. 1971) (emphasis added).

26. Costonis, *The Chicago Plan: Incentive Zoning and the Preservation of Urban Landmarks,* 85 HARV. L. REV. 574 (1972).

27. *See* People *ex rel.* Marbro Corp. v. Ramsey, 28 Ill. App. 2d 252, 171 N.E.2d 246 (1960); *In re* Opinion of the Justices, 333 Mass. 773, 128 N.E.2d 557 (1955).

28. *See* Costonis, *supra* note 26, *see also* Note, *Development Rights in New York City,* 82 YALE L.J. (338 (1972).

29. NEW YORK CITY ZONING ORDINANCE, art. VII, ch. 4, §§ 74-79 (1971) (emphasis added).

30. For a more detailed discussion of the system, *see* Note, *Building Size, Shape and Placement Regulations: Bulk Control Zoning Reexamined,* 60 YALE L.J. 506 (1951).

31. For discussion of the reasons for its failure, *see* Costonis, *supra* note 26, and Note, *Development Rights Transfer in New York City, supra* note 56.

32. SAN FRANCISCO CITY PLANNING CODE §§ 122-122.4.

33. *See* Sversky, *San Francisco: The Downtown Development Bonus System,* and Ruth, *Economic Aspects of the San Francisco Zoning Ordinance Bonus System,* both in THE NEW ZONING: LEGAL ADMINISTRATIVE AND ECONOMIC CONCEPTS AND TECHNIQUES (N. Marcus & M. Grove eds. 1970).

34. S. 254, Senate of Maryland; introduced, read first time and referred to the Committee on Economic Affairs, January, 1972.

35. Many of the provisions set forth herein contain modifications made by this author and may not be in accord with the corresponding provisions in the final draft submitted by the committee.

For a more detailed report of the work of this committee, see B. Chavooshian and T. Norman, Transfer of Development Rights: A New Concept in Land Use Management (Mimeo, Leaflet No. 492, Cooperative Extension Service, Cook College, Rutgers University, 1973).

36. *See* Rose, *Proposed Development Rights Legislation Can Change the Name of the Land Investment Game,* 1 REAL ESTATE L.J. 276 (1973).

Chapter 6
Allocation of Government Responsibility for Control
of Land Development

1. John J. Gibbons, "Senate Bill No. 803: Progress or Stagnation?" *Land Use Controls Quarterly* (Fall 1969), pp. 18-19.

2. State of New Jersey County and Municipal Government Study Commission, *County Government: Challenge and Change* (Trenton, N.J., 28 April 1969). For a brief summary of the findings, see pp. xvi-xxiv.

3. N.J. State Assembly Bill No. 1422.

4. Ibid., Article 13, p. 57.

5. N.J. State Assembly Bill No. 1422, Sec. 103.

6. National Commission on Urban Problems, *Building the American City* (Washington, D.C.: U.S. Government Printing Office, 1968), p. 39.

7. Sidney L. Willis and Thomas P. Norman, "New Jersey's Proposed Land Use Planning and Development Act," *Land Use Controls Quarterly* (Fall 1969), p. 10.

8. Laws of New Jersey, 1971, vol. 2 (1971), Sec. 2, c. 417, N.J. (approved Jan. 24, 1972).

9. Ibid., Sec. 3.

10. Ibid., Sec. 13b.

11. Laws of New Jersey, 1973, c. 185, N.J.

12. Maine Site Location of Development Act of 1970, as revised Sept. 1971.

13. Act No. 250 of the Vermont Laws of 1970, 10 Vt. Stat. Ann. c. 151, 556001, et seq.

14. *McKinney's N.Y. Consolidated Laws* (St. Paul, Minn.: West Publishing Co., 1971), General Municipal Law (Book 23), Sec. 239.

15. Report of the President: Committee on Urban Housing, *A Decent Home* (Washington, D.C.: U.S. Government Printing Office, 1968), pp. 143-44.

16. N.Y. State Urban Development Corporation, *McKinney's N.Y. Unconsolidated Laws* (St. Paul, Minn.: West Publishing Co., 1971), Sec. 6251, et. seq.

17. Massachusetts Acts (1969), c. 774 (c. 40-B, Secs. 20-23).

18. *Court Decision Upholding Chapter 774: A Summary*, a special report from the Citizens' Housing and Planning Association of Metropolitan Boston, 7 Marshall St., Boston, Mass., (May 1973).

19. Ibid., p. 5.

20. Frank Beal, "Massachusetts Takes Steps to Remove Local Barriers to Low-Income Housing," *Land Use Controls Quarterly* (Fall 1969), p. 33.

21. For a detailed description of the Kentucky legislation, see Tarlock, *Kentucky Planning and Land Use Control Enabling Legislation: An Analysis of the 1966 Revision of K.R.S. Chapter 100*, 56 KENTUCKY L.J., 556 (1968).

22. For a complete discussion of the Wisconsin legislation, see Donald F. Wood, "Wisconsin's Requirements for Shoreland and Flood Plain Protection," *Natural Resources Journal*, 10 (April 1970), 327.

23. National Commission on Urban Problems, *Building the American City*, op. cit., p. 236.

24. An Act Establishing a Metropolitan Council (unpublished draft prepared by Greater Boston Chamber of Commerce, 1973).

25. For an excellent, extensive analysis of the Hawaiian land-use planning, see Fred Bosselman and David Callief, *The Quiet Revolution in Land Use Contrcl*, prepared for the Council on Environmental Quality (Washington, D.C.: U.S. Government Printing Office, December 1971), pp. 5-53.

26. Office of State Planning, North Carolina Department of Administration, *Land Policy Alternatives for North Carolina* (Raleigh, N.C.: State of N.C., June 1972), pp. 106-108.

Chapter 7
Summary and Evaluation of the Techniques of
Land-Use Controls

1. See *Protection of Environmental Quality in Nonmetropolitan Regions by Limiting Development*, 57 IOWA L. REV. 126 (1971), particularly footnotes 4-14 for citations of articles describing this migration in different regions.

2. Ibid., p. 127.

3. In general, see *Techniques for Preserving Open Spaces*, 75 HARVARD L. REV. 1622 (1962); Eckert, Acquisition of Development Rights: A Modern Land Use Tool, 23 U. MIAMI L. REV. 347 (1969); Eveleth, *Appraisal of Techniques to Preserve Open Space*, 9 VILL. L. REV. 559 (1964); Beuscher, *Some Legal Aspects of Scenic Easement*, 1 LAND USE CONTROLS 28 (1967); Krasnowiecki and Paul, *The Preservation of Open Space in Metropolitan Areas*, 110 U. PA. L. REV. 179 (1961).

4. E. Freund, *The Police Power* (Chicago: Callaghan, 1904).

5. La Salle National Bank v. Chicago, 5 Ill. 2d 344, 350, 125 N.E. 2d 609, 612 (1955).

6. Robinson v. Town Council of Narragansett, 60 R.I. 422, 434, 199 A. 308, 313 (1938).

7. For a general discussion of this topic, see Heyman and Gilhool, *The Constitutionality of Imposing Increased Community Costs on New Suburban Residents Through Subdivision Extraction*, 73 YALE L.J. 119 (1964); Sax, *Takings and the Police Power*, 74 YALE L.J. 36 (1964); Netherton, *Implementation of Land Use Policy: Police Power vs. Eminent Domain*, 3 LAND AND WATER L. REV. 33 (1968); *Control of Urban Sprawl or Securing Open Space: Regulation by Condemnation or Ordinance?* 50 CAL. L. REV. 483 (1962).

8. See Jerome G. Rose, *Legal Foundations of Urban Planning: Cases and Materials on Planning Law* (New Brunswick, N.J.: Center for Urban Planning Policy Research, Rutgers University), 1973, p. 46.

9. Morris County Land Improvement Co. v. Parsippany-Troy Hills Township, 40 N.J. 539, 193 A. 2d 232 (1963).

10. Vernon Park Realty v. Mount Vernon, 307 N.Y. 493, 121 N.E.2d 517 (1954).

11. City of Plainfield v. Borough of Middlesex, 69 N.Y. *Supra* 136, 173 A.2d 785 (Law Div., 1961).

12. Greenhills Homeowners Corp. v. Village of Greenhills, 202 N.E.2d 192 Ohio Ct. App. (1964), rev'd. Ohio St.2d 207, 215 N.E.2d 403 (1965), cert. denied 385 U.S. 836 (1967); see Kusler, *Open Space Zoning: Valid Regulations or Invalid Taking*, 57 MINN. L. REV. 1 (1972).

13. Baker v. Planning Board, 353 Mass. 141, 228 N.E. 831 (1967). The Court held that a planning board could not disapprove a subdivision plan so that the town could continue to use the owner's land as a water storage area.

14. Morris County Land Improvement Co. v. Parsippany-Troy Hills Township, op. cit.

15. Ibid., p. 555.

16. Shoemaker v. United States, 147 U.S. 282 (1893).

17. N.J. Stat. Ann., Sec. 13:8A-1 (1961).

18. N.Y. Conservation Law, Secs. 1-07, 1-0708 (1960, as amended 1964).

19. 1B Mass. Laws. Ann. 40, Sec. 8(c) (1961).

20. Calif. Govt. Code 12, Secs. 6950-6954 (1959), Sec. 7000 (1963).

21. Wisc. Stat. Ann., Sec. 23.09(16).

22. For example, the Open Space Program in Title VII of the Housing Act of 1961, Secs. 701-06, 42 U.S.C.A., Secs. 1500-1500 (e) (Supp. 1961); the Federal Land and Water Conservation Program, 16 U.S.C., Secs. 4601-5 (Supp. V., 1970); the Cropland Adjustment Act, 7 U.S.C., Sec. 1838 (1971); the Watershed Protection and Flood Prevention Act, 16 U.S.C. Secs. 1001-09 (1964), as amended (Supp. V., 1970).

23. Krasnowiecki and Paul, op. cit., note 4; see also Jan Krasnowiecki and Ann Louise Strong, "Compensable Regulations for Open Space," *Journal of the American Institute of Planners*, 29 (1963), p. 87.

24. William H. Whyte, *Securing Open Space for Urban America: Conservation Easements*, Urban Land Inst. Tech. Bull. No. 36 (Washington, D.C.: Urban Land Institute, 1959).

25. N. Williams, *Land Acquisition for Outdoor-Recreation –Analysis of Selected Legal Problems* (Washington, D.C.: U.S.

Outdoor Recreation Resources Review Commission, 1963), Study Rept. 16, p. 48.

26. Ibid., p. 45.

27. H.R. Rep. No. 273, 87th Cong., 1st Sess. (1961), as cited in Eveleth, *An Appraisal of Techniques to Preserve Open Space*, 9 VILL. L. REV. 566-67 (1964), note 4.

Chapter 8
Conclusions and Recommendations

1. Adams, *The Land-Use Policy and Planning Assistance Act of 1973: Legislating a National Land Use Policy*, 41 GEORGE WASHINGTON L. REV. 609 (March 1973).

Appendix:
Draft of Development Rights Legislation with Commentary

1. See Cutler, *Legal and Illegal Methods for Controlling Community Growth on the Urban Fringe*, WISC. L. REV. 370 (1961).

Index

Index

139

140

acquisition, 34-35; acquisition of less than fee, 57, 58-59, 88-90; compensation vs. police power regulation, 86; conservation easements, 40-41, 58; constitutional issues, 31-32; and development rights transfer, 57, 58-59; excess condemnation, 39-40; land banking, 35-39; in New Jersey, 32-34, 58, 87; and open space acquisition, 31, 86-87; recommended legislation, 92; and the states, 58-59, 87; and urban renewal, 31, 34, 87, 90
Englewood, N.J., 16
Environmental impact statement (EIS), 28-30, 72, 92, 105-106; and taxation, 53-54. *See also* Regional land-use policy
"Equal protection," 20
Euclid v. *Ambler Realty* (1926), 7
Euclidian zoning, 7, 17, 20, 21
Exception process. *See* Variances
Excess condemnation, 39-40, 126 n.23, n.24
Exclusionary zoning, 8, 17-20, 26-27, 30, 67, 85; recommended legislation, 92, 93, 98
"Existing use" value, 57

FAR. *See* Floor-area ratio
FHA mortgage insurance programs, 83
"Fair share" regional housing policy, 93, 104
Farmland: acreage decline in New Jersey, 49, 127 n.8; and conservation easements, 89; dedication, 51-52; preferential tax assessment, 48-49, 51-53
Federal installations, 34-35
Federal land-use policy, vii, 7-9, 83; and eminent domain, 31, 34, 35, 38; and federal funding, 73, 78, 104; Land-Use Policy and Planning Assistance Act proposals, 95-96; and local governments, 76-77, 79; and urban renewal, 31, 34, 73
Fee simple. *See* Eminent domain acquisition
Fiscal Zoning, 85, 91. *See also* Municipal land-use policy
Fishing easements, 40
Floating value, 55, 56
Floating zones, 20-22, 92
Floor control, 14-15, 33-34, 79, 86. *See also* Wetlands
Floor-area ration (FAR): formula, 60; and incentive zoning transfer of FAR bonuses, 57, 61; and landmark transfer of FAR rights, 57, 59-61
Florida, vii; advance airport and highway land acquisition, 38, 39; contract zoning, 22; Environmental Land and Water Management Act (1972), 81-82

Fox-Lance formula, 50
Fragmentation of government authority. *See* Jurisdictional fragmentation

Gaffney, Mason, 46
"General welfare," 19
George, Henry, 43, 45, 48
Goertz, Margaret E., 1n
Golden v. *Planning Board of Town of Ramapo* (N.Y.S., 1972), 19, 92, 122 n.18
Goodman, William, 62
Government control of land development, allocation of, 65-82; and mandatory review, 73-76; in New Jersey, 66-73; and override of local land-use controls, 76-79; recommendations for, 92-93, 107; in states other than New Jersey, 73-82; and transfer of control to higher levels, 79-82. *See also* County, Federal, Municipal, Regional, State land-use policy
Graded property tax plan, 48
Great Britain: Barlow, Scott and Uthwatt Reports, 55-56; development rights transfer, 55-57, 129 n.8, n.12; land-use bibliography, 128 n.1, Town and County Planning Acts, 56-57
Great Depression, vii, 47
Greenbelt Movement, 34, 83n

HFA. *See* New Jersey Housing Finance Agency
HUD. *See* United States Department of Housing and Urban Development
Hackensack Meadows, N.J., 12-13, 70, 71, 99
Harvard Law Review, 28
Hawaii, vii, 66; advance land acquisition, 38; Board of Land and Natural Resources, 81; *City and County of Honolulu* v. *Bishop Trust Company* (1966), 32n; land-use classification and taxation, 51-52, 80-81, 92, 127 n.11; Land-Use Commission (LUC), 51, 80-81, 101; preferential farmland assessment, 51-52; transfer of development controls, 80-81, 98, 99
Highway land acquisition, 38-39
Historic sites, preservation of. *See* Landmark preservation
Home rule, 76, 79, 99; in New Jersey, 70, 71, 72, 97
Homestead Act (1862), 83
Honolulu, 32n
Hoover, Herbert, 7
Housing, low-income: and exclusionary zoning, 8, 17-20, 30, 67, 68; and "fair

About the Authors

Melvin R. Levin, Chairman of the Department of Urban Planning at Rutgers University, received the Ph.D. in planning from the University of Chicago. He has been a planning consultant and on the planning staff of agencies in New England, the Midwest, and the South as well as in New Jersey. He has also been a consultant to federal agencies, including the National Commission on Urban Problems. Professor Levin is the author of numerous books, including *Bureaucrats in Collision* (1970), *Community and Regional Planning* (1969, 1971), and *Exploring Urban Problems* (1971).

Jerome G. Rose is Professor of Urban Planning at Rutgers University; he received the J.D. from Harvard University School of Law. He is the editor of *Real Estate Law Journal* and has been a consultant to municipal and state agencies on zoning and land use matters. Professor Rose's recent books include *Landlords and Tenants: A Complete Guide to the Residential Rental Relationship* (1973), *Legal Foundations of Land Use Planning: Cases and Materials on Planning Law* (1974), and *Legal Foundations of Environmental Planning: Cases and Materials on Environmental Law* (1974).

Joseph S. Slavet is Director of the Boston Urban Observatory at the University of Massachusetts at Boston. A graduate of the Maxwell Graduate School of Citizenship and Public Affairs at Syracuse University, Mr. Slavet has been Professor of Urban Affairs at Boston University, the first Executive Director of Boston's anti-poverty agency, Executive Director of the Boston Municipal Research Bureau, and a consultant to municipal, state, and federal agencies, including the National Commission on Urban Problems. His major research works include two books coauthored with Melvin R. Levin: *Continuing Education* (1970) and *New Approaches to Housing Code Administration* (1968).